DOT1Q PUBLISHING

The Legislative Process

How Our Laws Are Made

Charles W. Johnson

Parliamentarian, U.S. House of Representatives

1/12/2010

Published by dot1q Publishing

ISBN: 978-0-9826266-0-3

First Printing 2010
Printed in the United States of America

Table of Contents

This page was intentionally left blank.

I

Introduction

This book is intended to provide a basic outline of the numerous steps of our federal lawmaking process from the source of an idea for a legislative proposal through its publication as a statute. The legislative process is a matter about which every person should be well informed in order to understand and appreciate the work of Congress.

It is hoped that this book will enable readers to gain a greater understanding of the federal legislative process and its role as one of the foundations of our representative system. One of the most practical safeguards of the American democratic way of life is this legislative process with its emphasis on the protection of the minority, allowing ample opportunity to all sides to be heard and make their views known. The fact that a proposal cannot become a law without consideration and approval by both Houses of Congress is an outstanding virtue of our bicameral legislative system. The open and full discussion provided under the Constitution often results in the notable improvement of a bill by amendment before it becomes law or in the eventual defeat of an inadvisable proposal.

As the majority of laws originate in the House of Representatives, this discussion will focus principally on the procedure in that body.

II

The Congress

Article I, Section 1, of the United States Constitution, provides that:

> All legislative Powers herein granted shall be vested in a Congress of the United States, which shall consist of a Senate and House of Representatives.

The Senate is composed of 100 Members—two from each state, regardless of population or area—elected by the people in accordance with the 17th Amendment to the Constitution. The 17th Amendment changed the former constitutional method under which Senators were chosen by the respective state legislatures. A Senator must be at least 30 years of age, have been a citizen of the United States for nine years, and, when elected, be a resident of the state for which the Senator is chosen. The term of office is six years and one-third of the total membership of the Senate is elected every second year. The terms of both Senators from a particular state are arranged so that they do not terminate at the same time. Of the two Senators from a state serving at the same time the one who was elected first—or if both were elected at the same time, the one elected for a full term—is referred to as the "senior" Senator from that state. The other is referred to as the "junior" Senator. If a Senator dies or resigns during the term, the governor of the state must call a special election unless the state legislature has authorized the governor to appoint a successor until the next election, at which time a successor is elected for the balance of the term. Most of the state legislatures have granted their governors the power of appointment.

Each Senator has one vote.

As constituted in the 108th Congress, the House of Representatives is composed of 435 Members elected every two years from among the 50 states, apportioned to their total populations. The permanent number of 435 was established by federal law following the Thirteenth Decennial Census in 1910, in accordance with Article I, Section 2, of the Constitution. This number was increased temporarily to 437 for the 87th Congress to provide for one Representative each for Alaska and Hawaii. The Constitution limits the number of Representatives to not more than one for every 30,000 of population. Under a former apportionment in one state, a particular Representative represented more than 900,000 constituents, while another in the same state was elected from a district having a population of only 175,000. The Supreme Court has since held unconstitutional a Missouri statute permitting a maximum population variance of 3.1 percent from mathematical equality. The Court ruled in *Kirkpatrick v. Preisler*, 394 U.S. 526 (1969), that the variances among the districts were not unavoidable and, therefore, were invalid. That decision was an interpretation of the Court's earlier ruling in *Wesberry v. Sanders*, 376 U.S. 1 (1964), that the Constitution requires that "as nearly as is practicable one man's vote in a congressional election is to be worth as much as another's".

A law enacted in 1967 abolished all "at-large" elections except in those less populous states entitled to only one Representative. An "at-large" election is one in which a Representative is elected by the voters of the entire state rather by the voters in a congressional district within a state.

A Representative must be at least 25 years of age, have been a citizen of the United States for seven years, and, when elected, be a resident of the state in which the Representative is chosen. Unlike the Senate where a successor may be appointed by a governor when a vacancy occurs during a term, if a Representative dies or resigns during the term, the executive authority of the state must call a special election pursuant to state law for the choosing of a successor to serve for the unexpired portion of the term.

Each Representative has one vote.

In addition to the Representatives from each of the States, a Resident Commissioner from the Commonwealth of Puerto Rico and Delegates from the District of

Columbia, American Samoa, Guam, and the Virgin Islands are elected pursuant to federal law. The Resident Commissioner, elected for a four-year term, and the Delegates, elected for two-year terms, have most of the prerogatives of Representatives including the right to vote in committees to which they are elected. However, the Resident Commissioner and the Delegates do not have the right to vote on matters before the House.

Under the provisions of Section 2 of the 20th Amendment to the Constitution, Congress must assemble at least once every year, at noon on the third day of January, unless by law they appoint a different day.

A Congress lasts for two years, commencing in January of the year following the biennial election of Members. A Congress is divided into two sessions.

The Constitution authorizes each House to determine the rules of its proceedings. Pursuant to that authority, the House of Representatives adopts its rules on the opening day of each Congress. The Senate considers itself a continuing body and operates under continuous standing rules that it amends from time to time.

Unlike some other parliamentary bodies, both the Senate and the House of Representatives have equal legislative functions and powers with certain exceptions. For example, the Constitution provides that only the House of Representatives originate revenue bills. By tradition, the House also originates appropriation bills. As both bodies have equal legislative powers, the designation of one as the "upper" House and the other as the "lower" House is not appropriate.

The chief function of Congress is the making of laws. In addition, the Senate has the function of advising and consenting to treaties and to certain nominations by the President. However under the 25th Amendment to the Constitution, both Houses confirm the President's nomination for Vice-President when there is a vacancy in that office. In the matter of impeachments, the House of Representatives presents the charges—a function similar to that of a grand jury—and the Senate sits as a court to try the impeachment. No impeached person may be removed without a two-thirds vote of the Senate. The Congress under the Constitution and by statute also plays a role in presidential elections. Both Houses meet in joint session on the sixth day of January, following a presidential election, unless by law they appoint a different day, to count the electoral votes. If no candidate receives a majority of the total electoral votes, the House of Representatives, each state delegation having one vote, chooses the President from among the three candidates having the largest number of electoral votes. The Senate, each Senator having one vote, chooses the Vice President from the two candidates having the largest number of votes for that office.

III

Sources of Legislation

Sources of ideas for legislation are unlimited and proposed drafts of bills originate in many diverse quarters. Primary among these is the idea and draft conceived by a Member. This may emanate from the election campaign during which the Member had promised, if elected, to introduce legislation on a particular subject. The Member may have also become aware after taking office of the need for amendment to or repeal of an existing law or the enactment of a statute in an entirely new field.

In addition, the Member's constituents, either as individuals or through citizen groups, may avail themselves of the right to petition and transmit their proposals to the Member. The right to petition is guaranteed by the First Amendment to the Constitution. Many excellent laws have originated in this way, as some organizations, because of their vital concern with various areas of legislation, have considerable knowledge regarding the laws affecting their interests and have the services of legislative draftspersons for this purpose. Similarly, state legislatures may "memorialize" Congress to enact specified federal laws by passing resolutions to be transmitted to the House and Senate as memorials. If favorably impressed by the idea, a Member may introduce the proposal in the form in which it has been submitted or may redraft it. In any event, a Member may consult with the Legislative Counsel of the House or the Senate to frame the ideas in suitable legislative language and form.

In modern times, the "executive communication" has become a prolific source of legislative proposals. The communication is usually in the form of a message or letter from a member of the President's Cabinet, the head of an independent agency, or the President himself, transmitting a draft of a proposed bill to the Speaker of the House of Representatives and the President of the Senate. Despite the structure of separation of powers, Article II, Section 3, of the Constitution imposes an obligation on the President to report to Congress from time to time on the "State of the Union" and to recommend for consideration such measures as the President considers necessary and expedient. Many of these executive communications follow on the President's message to Congress on the state of the Union. The communication is then referred to the standing committee or committees having jurisdiction of the subject matter of the proposal. The chairman or the ranking minority member of the relevant committee usually introduces the bill promptly either in the form in which it was received or with desired changes. This practice is usually followed even when the majority of the House and the President are not of the same political party, although there is no constitutional or statutory requirement that a bill be introduced to effectuate the recommendations. The committee or one of its subcommittees may also decide to examine the communication to determine whether a bill should be introduced. The most important of the regular executive communications is the annual message from the President transmitting the proposed budget to Congress. The President's budget proposal, together with testimony by officials of the various branches of the government before the Appropriations Committees of the House and Senate, is the basis of the several appropriation bills that are drafted by the Committee on Appropriations of the House.

Many of the executive departments and independent agencies employ legislative counsels who are charged with the drafting of bills. These legislative proposals are forwarded to Congress with a request for their enactment.

The drafting of statutes is an art that requires great skill, knowledge, and experience. In some instances, a draft is the result of a study covering a period of a year or more by a commission or committee designated by the President or a member of the Cabinet. The Administrative Procedure Act and the Uniform Code of Military Justice are two examples of enactments resulting from such studies. In addition, congressional committees sometimes draft bills after studies and hearings covering periods of a year or more.

IV

Forms of Congressional Action

The work of Congress is initiated by the introduction of a proposal in one of four forms: the bill, the joint resolution, the concurrent resolution, and the simple resolution. The most customary form used in both Houses is the bill. During the 107th Congress (2001–2002), 8,948 bills and 178 joint resolutions were introduced in both Houses. Of the total number introduced, 5,767 bills and 125 joint resolutions originated in the House of Representatives.

For the purpose of simplicity, this discussion will be confined generally to the procedure on a House of Representatives bill, with brief comment on each of the forms.

Bills

A bill is the form used for most legislation, whether permanent or temporary, general or special, public or private.

The form of a House bill is as follows:

A BILL

For the establishment, etc. [as the title may be].

Be it enacted by the Senate and House of Representatives of the United States of America in Congress assembled, That, etc.

The enacting clause was prescribed by law in 1871 and is identical in all bills, whether they originate in the House of Representatives or in the Senate.

Bills may originate in either the House of Representatives or the Senate with one notable exception provided for in the Constitution. Article I, Section 7, of the Constitution provides that all bills for raising revenue shall originate in the House of Representatives but that the Senate may propose or concur with amendments. By tradition, general appropriation bills also originate in the House of Representatives.

There are two types of bills—public and private. A public bill is one that affects the public generally. A bill that affects a specified individual or a private entity rather than the population at large is called a private bill. A typical private bill is used for relief in matters such as immigration and naturalization and claims against the United States.

A bill originating in the House of Representatives is designated by the letters "H.R." followed by a number that it retains throughout all its parliamentary stages. The letters signify “House of Representatives” and not, as is sometimes incorrectly assumed, “House resolution”. A Senate bill is designated by the letter “S.” followed by its number. The term “companion bill” is used to describe a bill introduced in one House of Congress that is similar or identical to a bill introduced in the other House of Congress.

A bill that has been agreed to in identical form by both bodies becomes the law of the land only after—

(1) Presidential approval; or

(2) Failure by the President to return it with objections to the House in which it originated within 10 days (Sundays excepted) while Congress is in session; or

(3) The overriding of a presidential veto by a two-thirds vote in each House.

It does not become law without the President’s signature if Congress by their final adjournment prevent its return with objections.

This is known as a “pocket veto”. For a discussion of presidential action on legislation, see Part XVIII.

JOINT RESOLUTIONS

Joint resolutions may originate either in the House of Representatives or in the Senate—not, as is sometimes incorrectly assumed, jointly in both Houses. There is little practical difference between a bill and a joint resolution and the two forms are often used interchangeably. One difference in form is that a joint resolution may include a preamble preceding the resolving clause. Statutes that have been initiated as bills have later been amended by a joint resolution and vice versa. Both are subject to the same procedure except for a joint resolution proposing an amendment to the Constitution. When a joint resolution amending the Constitution is approved by two-thirds of both Houses, it is not presented to the President for approval. Following congressional approval, a joint resolution to amend the Constitution is sent directly to the Archivist of the United States for submission to the several states where ratification by the legislatures of three-fourths of the states within the period of time prescribed in the joint resolution is necessary for the amendment to become part of the Constitution.

The form of a House joint resolution is as follows:

JOINT RESOLUTION

Authorizing, etc. [as the title may be].

Resolved by the Senate and House of Representatives of the United States of America in Congress assembled, That all, etc.

The resolving clause is identical in both House and Senate joint resolutions as prescribed by statute in 1871. It is frequently preceded by a preamble consisting of one or more "whereas" clauses indicating the necessity for or the desirability of the joint resolution.

A joint resolution originating in the House of Representatives is designated "H.J. Res." followed by its individual number, which it retains throughout all its parliamentary stages. One originating in the Senate is designated "S.J. Res." followed by its number.

Joint resolutions, with the exception of proposed amendments to the Constitution, become law in the same manner as bills.

Concurrent Resolutions

A matter affecting the operations of both Houses is usually initiated by a concurrent resolution. In modern practice, and as determined by the Supreme Court in *INS v. Chadha*, 462 U.S. 919 (1983), concurrent and simple resolutions normally are not legislative in character since not "presented" to the President for approval, but are used merely for expressing facts, principles, opinions, and purposes of the two Houses. A concurrent resolution is not equivalent to a bill and its use is narrowly limited within these bounds. The term "concurrent", like "joint", does not signify simultaneous introduction and consideration in both Houses.

A concurrent resolution originating in the House of Representatives is designated "H. Con. Res." followed by its individual number, while a Senate concurrent resolution is designated "S. Con. Res." together with its number. On approval by both Houses, they are signed by the Clerk of the House and the Secretary of the Senate and transmitted to the Archivist of the United States for publication in a special part of the Statutes at Large volume covering that session of Congress.

SIMPLE RESOLUTIONS

A matter concerning the rules, the operation, or the opinion of either House alone is initiated by a simple resolution. A resolution affecting the House of Representatives is designated "H. Res." followed by its number, while a Senate resolution is designated "S. Res." together with its number. Simple resolutions are considered only by the body in which they were introduced. Upon adoption, simple resolutions are attested to by the Clerk of the House of Representatives or the Secretary of the Senate and are published in the Congressional Record.

V

Introduction and Referral to Committee

Any Member, Delegate or the Resident Commissioner from Puerto Rico in the House of Representatives may introduce a bill at any time while the House is in session by simply placing it in the "hopper", a wooden box provided for that purpose located on the side of the rostrum in the House Chamber. Permission is not required to introduce the measure. The Member introducing the bill is known as the primary sponsor. An unlimited number of Members may cosponsor a bill. To prevent the possibility that a bill might be introduced in the House on behalf of a Member without that Member's prior approval, the primary sponsor's signature must appear on the bill before it is accepted for introduction. Members who cosponsor a bill upon its date of introduction are original cosponsors. Members who cosponsor a bill after its introduction are additional cosponsors. Cosponsors are not required to sign the bill. A Member may not be added or deleted as a cosponsor after the bill has been reported by the last committee authorized to consider it, but the Speaker may not entertain a request to delete the name of the primary sponsor at any time. Cosponsors names may be deleted by their own unanimous consent request or that of the primary sponsor. In the Senate, unlimited multiple sponsorship of a bill is permitted. Occasionally, a Member may insert the words "by request" after the Member's name to indicate that the introduction of the measure is at the suggestion of some other person or group—usually the President or a member of his Cabinet.

In the Senate, a Senator usually introduces a bill or resolution by presenting it to one of the clerks at the Presiding Officer's desk, without commenting on it from the floor of the Senate. However, a Senator may use a more formal procedure by rising and introducing the bill or resolution from the floor. A Senator usually makes a statement about the measure when introducing it on the floor. Frequently, Senators obtain consent to have the bill or resolution printed in the Congressional Record following their formal statement.

If any Senator objects to the introduction of a bill or resolution, the introduction of the bill or resolution is postponed until the next day. If there is no objection, the bill is read by title and referred to the appropriate committee. If there is an objection, the bill is placed on the Calendar.

In the House of Representatives, it is no longer the custom to read bills—even by title—at the time of introduction. The title is entered in the Journal and printed in the Congressional Record, thus preserving the purpose of the custom. The bill is assigned its legislative number by the Clerk. The bill is then referred as required by the rules of the House to the appropriate committee or committees by the Speaker, the Member elected by the Members to be the Presiding Officer of the House, with the assistance of the Parliamentarian. The bill number and committee referral appear in the next issue of the Congressional Record. It is then sent to the Government Printing Office where it is printed in its introduced form and printed copies are made available in the document rooms of both Houses. Printed and electronic versions of the bill are also made available to the public.

Copies of the bill are sent to the office of the chairman of the committee to which it has been referred. The clerk of the committee enters it on the committee's Legislative Calendar.

Perhaps the most important phase of the legislative process is the action by committees. The committees provide the most intensive consideration to a proposed measure as well as the forum where the public is given their opportunity to be heard. A tremendous volume of work, often overlooked by the public, is done by the Members in this phase. There are, at present, 19 standing committees in the House and 16 in the Senate as well as several select committees. In addition, there are four standing joint committees of the two Houses, with oversight responsibilities but no legislative jurisdiction. The House may also create select committees or task forces to study specific issues and report on them to the House. A task force may be established formally through a resolution passed by the House or informally through organization of interested Members by the House leadership.

Each committee's jurisdiction is divided into certain subject matters under the rules of each House and all measures affecting a particular area of the law are referred to the committee with jurisdiction over that particular subject matter. For example, the Committee on the Judiciary in the House has jurisdiction over measures relating to judicial proceedings generally, and 17 other categories, including constitutional amendments, immigration and naturalization, bankruptcy, patents, copyrights, and trademarks. In total, the rules of the House and of the Senate each provide for over 200 different classifications of measures to be referred to committees. Until 1975, the Speaker of the House could refer a bill to only one committee. In modern practice, the Speaker may refer the provisions of the bill within the jurisdiction of each committee concerned. Except in extraordinary circumstances, the Speaker must designate a primary committee of jurisdiction on bills referred to multiple committees. The Speaker may place time limits on the consideration of bills by all committees, but usually time limits are placed only on additional committees. Additional committees are committees other than the primary committee to which a bill has been referred, either initially on its introduction or sequentially following the report of the primary committee. A time limit is placed on an additional committee only when the primary committee has reported its version to the House.

Membership on the various committees is divided between the two major political parties. The proportion of the Members of the minority party to the Members of the majority party is determined by the majority party, except that half of the members on the Committee on Standards of Official Conduct are from the majority party and half from the minority party. The respective party caucuses nominate Members of the caucus to be elected to each standing committee at the beginning of each Congress. Membership on a standing committee during the course of a Congress is contingent on continuing membership in the party caucus that nominated a Member for election to the committee. If a Member ceases to be a Member of the party caucus, a Member automatically ceases to be a member of the standing committee.

Members of the House may serve on only two committees and four subcommittees with certain exceptions. However, the rules of the caucus of the majority party in the House provide that a Member may be chairman of only one subcommittee of a committee or select committee with legislative jurisdiction, except for certain committees performing housekeeping functions and joint committees.

A Member usually seeks election to the committee that has jurisdiction over a field in which the Member is most qualified and interested. For example, the Committee on the Judiciary traditionally is composed almost entirely of lawyers. Many Members are nationally recognized experts in the specialty of their particular committee or subcommittee.

Members rank in seniority in accordance with the order of their appointment to the full committee and the ranking majority member with the most continuous service is usually elected chairman. The rules of the House require that committee chairmen be elected from nominations submitted by the majority party caucus at the commencement of each Congress. In the 108th Congress, no Member of the House may serve as chairman of the same standing committee or of the same subcommittee thereof for more than three consecutive Congresses.

The rules of the House prohibit a committee that maintains a subcommittee on oversight from having more than six subcommittees with the exception of the Committee on Appropriations and the Committee on Government Reform.

Each committee is provided with a professional staff to assist it in the innumerable administrative details involved in the consideration of bills and its oversight responsibilities. For standing committees, the professional staff is limited to 30 persons appointed by a vote of the committee. Two-thirds of the committee staff are selected by a majority vote of the majority committee members and one-third of the committee staff are selected by a majority vote of minority committee members. All staff appointments are made without regard to race, creed, sex, or age. Minority staff requirements do not apply to the Committee on Standards of Official Conduct because of its bipartisan nature. The Committee on Appropriations has special authority under the rules of the House for appointment of staff for the minority.

VI

Consideration by Committee

One of the first actions taken by a committee is to seek the input of the relevant departments and agencies about a bill. Frequently, the bill is also submitted to the General Accounting Office with a request for an official report of views on the necessity or desirability of enacting the bill into law. Normally, ample time is given for the submission of the reports and they are accorded serious consideration. However, these reports are not binding on the committee in determining whether or not to act favorably on the bill. Reports of the departments and agencies in the executive branch are submitted first to the Office of Management and Budget to determine whether they are consistent with the program of the President. Many committees adopt rules requiring referral of measures to the appropriate subcommittee unless the full committee votes to retain the measure at the full committee.

Committee Meetings

Standing committees are required to have regular meeting days at least once a month. The chairman of the committee may also call and convene additional meetings. Three or more members of a standing committee may file with the committee a written request that the chairman call a special meeting. The request must specify the measure or matter to be considered. If the chairman does not call the requested special meeting within three calendar days after the filing of the request, to be held within seven calendar days after the filing of the request, a majority of the members of the committee may call the special meeting by filing with the committee written notice specifying the date, hour, and the measure or matter to be considered at the meeting. In the Senate, the Chair may still control the agenda of the special meeting through the power of recognition. Committee meetings may be held for various purposes including the "markup" of legislation, authorizing subpoenas, or internal budget and personnel matters.

A subpoena may be authorized and issued at a meeting by a vote of a committee or subcommittee with a majority of members present. The power to authorize and issue subpoenas also may be delegated to the chairman of the committee. A subpoena may require both testimonial and documentary evidence to be furnished to the committee. A subpoena is signed by the chairman of the committee or by a member designated by the committee.

All meetings for the transaction of business of standing committees or subcommittees, except the Committee on Standards of Official Conduct, must be open to the public, except when the committee or subcommittee, in open session with a majority present, determines by record vote that all or part of the remainder of the meeting on that day shall be closed to the public. Members of the committee may authorize congressional staff and departmental representatives to be present at any meeting that has been closed to the public. Open committee meetings may be covered by the media. Permission to cover hearings and meetings is granted under detailed conditions as provided in the rules of the House.

The rules of the House provide that House committees may not meet during a joint session of the House and Senate or during a recess when a joint meeting of the House and Senate is in progress. Committees may meet at other times during an adjournment or recess up to the expiration of the constitutional term.

Public Hearings

If the bill is of sufficient importance, the committee may set a date for public hearings. The chairman of each committee, except for the Committee on Rules, is required to make public announcement of the date, place, and subject matter of any hearing at least one week before the commencement of that hearing, unless the committee chairman with the concurrence of the ranking minority member or the committee by majority vote determines that there is good cause to begin the hearing at an earlier date. If that determination is made, the chairman must make a public announcement to that effect at the earliest possible date. Public announcements are published in the Daily Digest portion of the Congressional Record as soon as possible after an announcement is made and are often noted by the media. Personal notice of the hearing, usually in the form of a letter, is sometimes sent to relevant individuals, organizations, and government departments and agencies.

Each hearing by a committee or subcommittee, except the Committee on Standards of Official Conduct, is required to be open to the public except when the committee or subcommittee, in open session and with a majority present, determines by record vote that all or part of the remainder of the hearing on that day shall be closed to the public because disclosure of testimony, evidence, or other matters to be considered would endanger national security, would compromise sensitive law enforcement information, or would violate a law or a rule of the House. The committee or subcommittee may by the same procedure vote to close one subsequent day of hearing, except that the Committees on Appropriations, Armed Services, and the Permanent Select Committee on Intelligence, and subcommittees thereof, may vote to close up to five additional, consecutive days of hearings. When a quorum for taking testimony is present, a majority of the members present may close a hearing to discuss whether the evidence or testimony to be received would endanger national security or would tend to defame, degrade, or incriminate any person. A committee or subcommittee may vote to release or make public matters originally received in a closed hearing or meeting. Open committee hearings may be covered by the media. Permission to cover hearings and meetings is granted under detailed conditions as provided in the rules of the House.

Hearings on the Budget are required to be held by the Committee on Appropriations in open session within 30 days after its transmittal to Congress, except when the committee, in open session and with a quorum present, determines by record vote that the testimony to be taken at that hearing on that day may be related to a matter of national security. The committee may by the same procedure close one subsequent day of hearing.

On the day set for a public hearing in a committee or subcommittee, an official reporter is present to record the testimony. After a brief introductory statement by the chairman and often by the ranking minority member or other committee member, the first witness is called. Members or Senators who wish to be heard sometimes testify first out of courtesy and due to the limitations on their time. Cabinet officers and high-ranking government officials, as well as interested private individuals, testify either voluntarily or by subpoena.

So far as practicable, committees require that witnesses who appear before it file a written statement of their proposed testimony in advance of their appearance and limit their oral presentations to a brief summary of their arguments. In the case of a witness appearing in a nongovernmental capacity, a written statement of proposed testimony shall include a curriculum vitae and a disclosure of certain federal grants and contracts.

Minority party members of the committee are entitled to call witnesses of their own to testify on a measure during at least one additional day of a hearing.

Each member of the committee is provided only five minutes in the interrogation of each witness until each member of the committee who desires to question a witness has had an opportunity to do so. In addition, a committee may adopt a rule or motion to permit committee members to question a witness for a specified period not longer than one hour. Committee staff may also be permitted to question a witness for a specified period not longer than one hour.

A transcript of the testimony taken at a public hearing is made available for inspection in the office of the clerk of the committee. Frequently, the complete transcript is printed and distributed widely by the committee.

Markup

After hearings are completed, the subcommittee usually will consider the bill in a session that is popularly known as the "markup" session. The views of both sides are studied in detail and at the conclusion of deliberation a vote is taken to determine the action of the subcommittee. It may decide to report the bill favorably to the full committee, with or without amendment, or unfavorably, or without recommendation. The subcommittee may also suggest that the committee "table" it or postpone action indefinitely. Each member of the subcommittee, regardless of party affiliation, has one vote. Proxy voting is no longer permitted in House committees.

FINAL COMMITTEE ACTION

At full committee meetings, reports on bills may be made by subcommittees. Bills are read for amendment in committees by section and members may offer germane amendments. Committee amendments are only proposals to change the bill as introduced and are subject to acceptance or rejection by the House itself. A vote of committee members is taken to determine whether the full committee will report the bill favorably, adversely, or without recommendation. If the committee votes to report the bill favorably to the House, it may report the bill without amendments or may introduce and report a "clean bill". Committees may authorize the chairman to postpone votes in certain circumstances. If the committee has approved extensive amendments, the committee may decide to report the original bill with one "amendment in the nature of a substitute" consisting of all the amendments previously adopted, or may report a new bill incorporating those amendments, commonly known as a clean bill. The new bill is introduced (usually by the chairman of the committee), and, after referral back to the committee, is reported favorably to the House by the committee. A committee may table a bill or not take action on it, thereby preventing further action on a bill. This makes adverse reports or reports without recommendation to the House by a committee unusual. The House also has the ability to discharge a bill from committee. For a discussion of the motion to discharge, see Part X.

Generally, a majority of the committee or subcommittee constitutes a quorum. A quorum is the number of members who must be present in order for the committee to report. This ensures participation by both sides in the action taken. However, a committee may vary the number of members necessary for a quorum for certain actions. For example, a committee may fix the number of its members, but not less than two, necessary for a quorum for taking testimony and receiving evidence. Except for the Committees on Appropriations, the Budget, and Ways and Means, a committee may fix the number of its members, but not less than one-third, necessary for a quorum for taking certain other actions. The absence of a quorum is subject to a point of order, an objection that the proceedings are in violation of a rule of the committee or of the House, because the required number of members are not present.

Points of Order with Respect to Committee Hearing Procedure

A point of order in the House does not lie with respect to a measure reported by a committee on the ground that hearings on the measure were not conducted in accordance with required committee procedure. However, certain points of order may be made by a member of the committee that reported the measure if, in the committee hearing on that measure, that point of order was (1) timely made and (2) improperly disposed of.

VII

Reported Bills

If the committee votes to report the bill to the House, the committee staff writes a committee report. The report describes the purpose and scope of the bill and the reasons for its recommended approval. Generally, a section-by-section analysis is set forth explaining precisely what each section is intended to accomplish. All changes in existing law must be indicated in the report and the text of laws being repealed must be set out. This requirement is known as the "Ramseyer" rule. A similar rule in the Senate is known as the "Cordon" rule. Committee amendments also must be set out at the beginning of the report and explanations of them are included. Executive communications regarding the bill may be referenced in the report.

If at the time of approval of a bill by a committee, except for the Committee on Rules, a member of the committee gives notice of an intention to file supplemental, minority, or additional views, that member is entitled to not less than two additional calendar days after the day of such notice (excluding Saturdays, Sundays, and legal holidays unless the House is in session on those days) in which to file those views with the clerk of the committee. Those views that are timely filed must be included in the report on the bill. Committee reports must be filed while the House is in session unless unanimous consent is obtained from the House to file at a later time or the committee is awaiting additional views.

The report is assigned a report number upon its filing and is sent to the Government Printing Office for printing. House reports are given a prefix-designator that indicates the number of the Congress. For example, the first House report in the 108th Congress was numbered 108–1.

In the printed report, committee amendments are indicated by showing new matter in italics and deleted matter in line-through type. The report number is printed on the bill and the calendar number is shown on both the first and back pages of the bill. However, in the case of a bill that was referred to two or more committees for consideration in sequence, the calendar number is printed only on the bill as reported by the last committee to consider it. For a discussion of House calendars, see Part IX.

Committee reports are perhaps the most valuable single element of the legislative history of a law. They are used by the courts, executive departments, and the public as a source of information regarding the purpose and meaning of the law.

Contents of Reports

The report of a committee on a measure that has been approved by the committee must include: (1) the committee's oversight findings and recommendations; (2) a statement required by the Congressional Budget Act of 1974, if the measure is a bill or joint resolution providing new budget authority (other than continuing appropriations) or an increase or decrease in revenues or tax expenditures; (3) a cost estimate and comparison prepared by the Director of the Congressional Budget Office whenever the Director has submitted that estimate and comparison to the committee prior to the filing of the report; and (4) a statement of general performance goals and objectives, including outcome-related goals and objectives, for which the measure authorizes funding. Each report accompanying a bill or joint resolution relating to employment or access to public services or accommodations must describe the manner in which the provisions apply to the legislative branch. Each of these items are set out separately and clearly identified in the report.

With respect to each record vote by a committee, the total number of votes cast for, and the total number of votes cast against any public measure or matter or amendment thereto and the names of those voting for and against, must be included in the committee report.

In addition, each report of a committee on a public bill or public joint resolution must contain a statement citing the specific powers granted to Congress in the Constitution to enact the law proposed by the bill or joint resolution. Committee reports that accompany bills or resolutions that contain federal unfunded mandates are also required to include an estimate prepared by the Congressional Budget Office on the cost of the mandates on state, local, and tribal governments. If an estimate is not available at the time a report is filed, committees are required to publish the estimate in the Congressional Record. Each report also must contain an estimate, made by the committee, of the costs which would be incurred in carrying out that bill or joint resolution in the fiscal year reported and in each of the five fiscal years thereafter or for the duration of the program authorized if less than five years. The report must include a comparison of the estimates of those costs with any estimate made by any Government agency and submitted to that committee. The Committees on Appropriations, House Administration, Rules, and Standards of Official Conduct are not required to include cost estimates in their reports. In addition, the committee's own cost estimates are not required to be included in reports when Congressional Budget Office has been submitted prior to the filing of the report and included in the report.

Filing of Reports

Measures approved by a committee must be reported by the Chairman promptly after approval. If not, a majority of the members of the committee may file a written request with the clerk of the committee for the reporting of the measure. When the request is filed, the clerk must immediately notify the chairman of the committee of the filing of the request, and the report on the measure must be filed within seven calendar days (excluding days on which the House is not in session) after the day on which the request is filed. This does not apply to a report of the Committee on Rules with respect to a rule, joint rule, or order of business of the House or to the reporting of a resolution of inquiry addressed to the head of an executive department.

Availability of Reports and Hearings

A measure or matter reported by a committee (except the Committee on Rules in the case of a resolution providing a rule, joint rule, or order of business) may not be considered in the House until the third calendar day (excluding Saturdays, Sundays, and legal holidays unless the House is in session on those days) on which the report of that committee on that measure has been available to the Members of the House. This rule is subject to certain exceptions including resolutions providing for certain privileged matters and measures declaring war or other national emergency. However, it is in order to consider a report from the Committee on Rules on the same day it is reported that proposes only to waive this availability requirement. If hearings were held on a measure or matter so reported, the committee is required to make every reasonable effort to have those hearings printed and available for distribution to the Members of the House prior to the consideration of the measure in the House. Committees are also required, to the maximum extent feasible, to make their publications available in electronic form. A general appropriation bill reported by the Committee on Appropriations may not be considered until printed committee hearings and a committee report thereon have been available to the Members of the House for at least three calendar days (excluding Saturdays, Sundays, and legal holidays unless the House is in session on those days).

VIII

Legislative Oversight by Standing Committees

Each standing committee, other than the Committees on Appropriations and on the Budget, is required to review and study, on a continuing basis, the application, administration, execution, and effectiveness of the laws dealing with the subject matter over which the committee has jurisdiction and the organization and operation of federal agencies and entities having responsibility for the administration and evaluation of those laws.

The purpose of the review and study is to determine whether laws and the programs created by Congress are being implemented and carried out in accordance with the intent of Congress and whether those programs should be continued, curtailed, or eliminated. In addition, each committee having oversight responsibility is required to review and study any conditions or circumstances that may indicate the necessity or desirability of enacting new or additional legislation within the jurisdiction of that committee, and must undertake, on a continuing basis, future research and forecasting on matters within the jurisdiction of that committee. Each standing committee also has the function of reviewing and studying, on a continuing basis, the impact or probable impact of tax policies on subjects within its jurisdiction.

The rules of the House provide for special treatment of an investigative or oversight report of a committee. Committees are allowed to file joint investigative reports and to file investigative and activities reports after the House has completed its final session of a Congress. In addition, several of the standing committees have special oversight responsibilities. The details of those responsibilities are set forth in the rules of the House.

IX

CALENDARS

The House of Representatives has five calendars of business: the Union Calendar, the House Calendar, the Private Calendar, the Corrections Calendar, and the Calendar of Motions to Discharge Committees. The calendars are compiled in one publication printed each day the House is in session. This publication also contains a history of Senate-passed bills, House bills reported out of committee, bills on which the House has acted, and other useful information.

When a public bill is favorably reported by all committees to which referred, it is assigned a calendar number on either the Union Calendar or the House Calendar, the two principal calendars of business. The calendar number is printed on the first page of the bill and, in certain instances, is printed also on the back page. In the case of a bill that was referred to multiple committees for consideration in sequence, the calendar number is printed only on the bill as reported by the last committee to consider it.

UNION CALENDAR

The rules of the House provide that there shall be:

> A Calendar of the Committee of the Whole House on the state of the Union, to which shall be referred public bills and public resolutions raising revenue, involving a tax or charge on the people, directly or indirectly making appropriations of money or property or requiring such appropriations to be made, authorizing payments out of appropriations already made, releasing any liability to the United States for money or property, or referring a claim to the Court of Claims.

The large majority of public bills and resolutions reported to the House are placed on the Union Calendar. For a discussion of the Committee of the Whole House, see Part XI.

HOUSE CALENDAR

The rules further provide that there shall be:

> A House Calendar, to which shall be referred all public bills and public resolutions not requiring referral to the Calendar of the Committee of the Whole House on the state of the Union.

Bills not involving a cost to the government and resolutions providing special orders of business are examples of bills and resolutions placed on the House Calendar.

PRIVATE CALENDAR

The rules also provide that there shall be:

> A Private Calendar,...to which shall be referred all private bills and private resolutions.

All private bills reported to the House are placed on the Private Calendar. The Private Calendar is called on the first and third Tuesdays of each month. If two or more Members object to the consideration of any measure called, it is recommitted to the committee that reported it. There are six official objectors, three on the majority side and three on the minority side, who make a careful study of each bill or resolution on the Private Calendar. The official objectors' role is to object to a measure that does not conform to the requirements for that calendar and prevent the passage without debate of nonmeritorious bills and resolutions. Private bills that have been reported from committee are only considered under the private calendar procedure. Alternative procedures reserved for public bills are not applicable for reported private bills.

CORRECTIONS CALENDAR

If a measure pending on either the House or Union Calendar is of a noncontroversial nature, it may be placed on the Corrections Calendar. The Corrections Calendar was created to address specific problems with federal rules, regulations, or court decisions that bipartisan and narrowly targeted bills could expeditiously correct. After a bill has been favorably reported and is on either the House or Union Calendar, the Speaker may, after consultation with the Minority Leader, file with the Clerk a notice requesting that such bill also be placed upon a special calendar known as the Corrections Calendar. On the second and fourth Tuesdays of each month, the Speaker directs the Clerk to call any bill that has been printed on the Corrections Calendar. A three-fifths vote of the Members voting is required to pass any bill called from the Corrections Calendar. A failure to adopt a bill from the Corrections Calendar does not necessarily mean the final defeat of the bill because it may then be brought up for consideration in the same way as any other bill on the House or Union Calendar.

Calendar of Motions to Discharge Committees

When a majority of the Members of the House sign a motion to discharge a committee from consideration of a public bill or resolution, that motion is referred to the Calendar of Motions to Discharge Committees. For a discussion of the motion to discharge, see Part X.

X

Obtaining Consideration of Measures

Certain measures, either pending on the House and Union Calendars or unreported and pending in committee, are more important and urgent than others and a system permitting their consideration ahead of those that do not require immediate action is necessary. If the calendar numbers alone were the determining factor, the bill reported most recently would be the last to be taken up as all measures are placed on the House and Union Calendars in the order reported.

Unanimous Consent

The House occasionally employs the practice of allowing reported or unreported measures to be considered by the unanimous agreement of all Members in the

House Chamber. The power to recognize Members for a unanimous consent request is ultimately in the discretion of the Chair but recent Speakers have issued strict guidelines on when such a request is to be entertained. Most unanimous consent requests for consideration of measures may only be entertained by the Chair when assured that the majority and minority floor and committee leaderships have no objection.

SPECIAL RESOLUTION OR "RULE"

To avoid delays and to allow selectivity in the consideration of public measures, it is possible to have them taken up out of their order on their respective calendar or to have them discharged from the committee or committees to which referred by obtaining from the Committee on Rules a special resolution or "rule" for their consideration. The Committee on Rules, which is composed of majority and minority members but with a larger proportion of majority members than other committees, is specifically granted jurisdiction over resolutions relating to the order of business of the House. Typically, the chairman of the committee that has favorably reported the bill requests the Committee on Rules to originate a resolution that will provide for its immediate or subsequent consideration. Under some circumstances, the Committee on Rules may originate a resolution providing for the "discharge" and consideration of a measure that has not been reported by the legislative committee or committees of jurisdiction. If the Committee on Rules has determined that the measure should be taken up, it may report a resolution reading substantially as follows with respect to a bill on the Union Calendar or an unreported bill:

> *Resolved,* That upon the adoption of this resolution the Speaker declares pursuant to rule XVIII that the House resolve itself into the Committee of the Whole House on the State of the Union for the consideration of the bill (H.R.________) entitled, etc., and the first reading of the bill shall be dispensed with. After general debate, which shall be confined to the bill and shall continue not to exceed ________ hours, to be equally divided and controlled by the chairman and ranking minority member of the Committee on ________, the bill shall be read for amendment under the five-minute rule. At the conclusion of the consideration of the bill for amendment, the Committee shall rise and report the bill to the House with such amendments as may have been adopted, and the previous question shall be considered as ordered on the bill and amendments thereto to final passage without intervening motion except one motion to recommit with or without instructions.

If the measure is on the House Calendar or the recommendation is to avoid consideration in the Committee of the Whole, the resolution reads substantially as follows:

> *Resolved,* That upon the adoption of this resolution it shall be in order to consider the bill (H.R.________) entitled, etc., in the House.

The resolution may waive points of order against the bill. A point of order is an objection that a pending matter or proceeding is in violation of a rule of the House. The bill may be susceptible to various points of order that may be made against its consideration, including an assertion that the bill carries a retroactive federal income tax increase, contains a federal unfunded mandate, or has not been reported from committee properly. At times, the rule may "self-execute" changes to the bill, that is, incorporate the changes in the bill upon adoption of the rule. The rule may also make a specified "manager's amendment" in order prior to any other amendment or may make a "compromise substitute" amendment in order as original text to replace the version reported from committee. When a rule limits or prevents floor amendments, it is popularly known as a "closed rule" or "modified closed rule." However, a rule may not deny the minority party the right to offer a motion to recommit the bill with proper amendatory or general instructions. For a discussion of the motion to recommit, see Part XI.

Consideration of Measures Made in Order by Rule Reported from the Committee on Rules

When a rule has been reported to the House, it is referred veto the calendar and if it is to be considered immediately on the same legislative day reported, it requires a two-thirds vote for its consideration. Normally, however, the rule is on the calendar for at least one legislative day and if not called up for consideration by the

Member who filed the report within seven legislative days thereafter, any member of the Committee on Rules may call it up as a privileged matter, after having given one calendar day notice of the Member's intention to do so. The Speaker will recognize any member of the committee seeking recognition for that purpose.

If the House has adopted a resolution making in order a motion to consider a bill, and such a motion has not been offered within seven calendar days thereafter, such a motion shall be privileged if offered by direction of all reporting committees having initial jurisdiction of the bill.

There are several other methods of obtaining consideration of bills that either have not been reported by a committee or, if reported, for which a rule has not been granted. Two of those methods, a motion to discharge a committee and a motion to suspend the rules, are discussed below.

Motion to Discharge Committee

A Member may present to the Clerk a motion in writing to discharge a committee from the consideration of a public bill or resolution that has been referred to it 30 legislative days prior thereto. A Member also may file a motion to discharge the Committee on Rules from further consideration of a resolution providing a special rule for the consideration of a public bill or resolution reported by a standing committee, or a special rule for the consideration of a public bill or resolution that has been referred to a standing committee for 30 legislative days. This motion to discharge the Committee on Rules may be made only when the resolution has been referred to that committee at least seven legislative days prior to the filing of the motion to discharge. The motion may not permit consideration of nongermane amendments. The motion is placed in the custody of the Journal Clerk, where Members may sign it at the House rostrum only when the House is in session. The names of Members who have signed a discharge motion are made available electronically and published in the Congressional Record on a weekly basis. When a majority of the total membership of the House (218 Members) have signed the motion, it is entered in the Journal, printed with all the signatures thereto in the Congressional Record, and referred to the Calendar of Motions to Discharge Committees.

On the second and fourth Mondays of each month, except during the last six days of a session, a Member who has signed a motion to discharge that has been on the calendar at least seven legislative days may seek recognition and be recognized for the purpose of calling up the motion. The motion to discharge is debated for 20 minutes, one-half in favor of the proposition and one-half in opposition.

If the motion to discharge the Committee on Rules from a resolution prevails, the House shall immediately consider such resolution. If the resolution is adopted, the House proceeds to its execution. This is the modern practice for utilization of the discharge rule.

If the motion to discharge a standing committee of the House from a public bill or resolution pending before the committee prevails, a Member who signed the motion may move that the House proceed to the immediate consideration of the bill or resolution. If the motion is agreed to, the bill or resolution is considered immediately under the general rules of the House. If the House votes against the motion for immediate consideration, the bill or resolution is referred to its proper calendar with the same status as if reported by a standing committee.

Motion to Suspend the Rules

On Monday and Tuesday of each week and during the last six days of a session, the Speaker may entertain a motion to suspend the rules of the House and pass a public bill or resolution. Sometimes the motion is allowed on days other than Monday and Tuesday by unanimous consent or a rule from the Committee on Rules. For example, the House by rule from the Committee on Rules provided for the motion on Wednesdays for the remainder of the 108th Congress. Members need to arrange in advance with the Speaker to be recognized to offer such a motion. The Speaker usually recognizes only a majority member of the committee that has reported or has primary jurisdiction over the bill. The motion to suspend the rules and pass the bill is debatable for 40 minutes, one-half of the time in favor of the proposition and one-half in opposition. The motion may not be separately amended but may be amended in the form of a manager's amendment included in the motion when it is offered. Because the rules may be suspended and the bill passed only by affirmative vote of two-thirds of the Members voting, a quorum being present, this procedure is usually used only for expedited consideration of relatively noncontroversial public measures.

The Speaker may postpone all recorded and yea-nay votes on certain questions before the House, including a motion to suspend the rules and on passage of bills and resolutions, until a specified time or times on that legislative day or the next two legislative days. At these times, the House disposes of the postponed votes consecutively without further debate. After an initial fifteen-minute vote is taken, the Speaker may reduce to not less than five minutes the time period for subsequent votes. Eliminating intermittent recorded votes on suspensions reduces interruptions of committee activity and allows more efficient scheduling of voting.

CALENDAR WEDNESDAY

On Wednesday of each week, unless dispensed with by unanimous consent or by affirmative vote of two-thirds of the Members voting, a quorum being present, the standing committees are called in alphabetical order. A committee when named may call up for consideration any bill reported by it on a previous day and pending on either the House or Union Calendar. The report on the bill must have been available for three days and must not be privileged under the rules of the House. General debate is limited to two hours on any Calendar Wednesday measure and must be confined to the subject matter of the measure, the time being equally divided between those for and those against. An affirmative vote of a simple majority of the Members present is sufficient to pass the measure. The purpose of this rarely utilized procedure is to provide an alternative method of consideration when the Committee on Rules has not reported a rule for a specific bill.

District of Columbia Business

On the second and fourth Mondays of each month, after the disposition of motions to discharge committees and after the disposal of business on the Speaker's table requiring only referral to committee, the Committee on Government Reform may call up for consideration any District of Columbia business reported from that committee. This procedure is rarely utilized in the modern House.

Questions of Privilege

House rules provide special privilege to questions of privilege. Questions of privilege are classified as those questions: (1) affecting the rights of the House collectively, its safety, dignity, and the integrity of its proceedings; and (2) affecting the rights, reputations, and conduct of Members, individually, in their representative capacity. A question of privilege has been held to take precedence over all questions except the motion to adjourn. Questions of the privileges of the House, those concerning the rights of the House collectively, take the form of a resolution which may be called up by any Member after proper notice. A question of personal privilege, affecting the rights, reputation, and conduct of individual Members, may be raised from the floor without formal notice. Debate on a question of privilege proceeds under the hour rule, with debate on a question of the privileges of the House divided between the proponent and the leader of the opposing party or a designee.

PRIVILEGED MATTERS

Under the rules of the House, certain matters are regarded as privileged matters and may interrupt the order of business. Conference reports, veto messages from the President, and certain amendments to measures by the Senate after the stage of disagreement between the two Houses are examples of privileged matters. Certain reports from House committees are also privileged, including reports from the Committee on Rules, reports from the Committee on Appropriations on general appropriation bills, printing and committee funding resolutions reported from the Committee on House Administration, and reports on Member's conduct from the Committee on Standards of Official Conduct. Bills, joint resolutions, and motions may also take on privileged status as a result of special procedures written into statute. The Member in charge of such a matter may call it up at practically any time for immediate consideration when no other business is pending. Usually, this is done after consultation with both the majority and minority floor leaders so that the Members of both parties will have advance notice.

At any time after the reading of the Journal, a Member, by direction of the Committee on Appropriations, may move that the House resolve itself into the Committee of the Whole House on the state of the Union for the purpose of considering a general appropriation bill. A general appropriation bill may not be considered in the House until three calendar days (excluding Saturdays, Sundays, and legal holidays unless the House is in session on those days) after printed committee reports and hearings on the bill have been available to the Members. The limit on general debate on such a bill is generally fixed by a rule reported from the Committee on Rules.

XI

Consideration and Debate

Our democratic tradition demands that bills be given consideration by the entire membership usually with adequate opportunity for debate and the proposing of amendments.

Committee of the Whole

In order to expedite the consideration of bills and resolutions, the rules of the House provide for a parliamentary mechanism, known as the Committee of the Whole House on the state of the Union, that enables the House to act with a quorum of less than the requisite majority of 218. A quorum in the Committee of the Whole is 100 members. All measures on the Union Calendar—those involving a tax, making appropriations, authorizing payments out of appropriations already made, or disposing of property—must be first considered in the Committee of the Whole.

The Committee on Rules reports a rule allowing for immediate consideration of a measure by the Committee of the Whole. After adoption of the rule by the House, the Speaker may declare the House resolved into the Committee of the Whole. When the House resolves into the Committee of the Whole, the Speaker leaves the chair after appointing a Chairman to preside.

The rule referred to in the preceding paragraph also fixes the length of the debate in the Committee of the Whole. This may vary according to the importance of the measure. As provided in the rule, the control of the time is usually divided equally between the chairman and the ranking minority member of the relevant committee. Members seeking to speak for or against the measure may arrange in advance with the Member in control of the time on their respective side to be allowed a certain amount of time in the debate. Members may also ask the Member speaking at the time to yield to them for a question or a brief statement. A transcript of the proceedings in the House and the Senate is printed daily in the Congressional Record. Frequently, permission is granted a Member by unanimous consent to revise and extend his remarks in the Congressional Record if sufficient time to make a lengthy oral statement is not available during actual debate. These revisions and extensions are printed in a distinctive type and cannot substantively alter the verbatim transcript.

The conduct of the debate is governed principally by the rules of the House that are adopted at the opening of each Congress. In the 106th Congress, the rules were recodified for simplification and clarity. *Jefferson's Manual,* prepared by Thomas Jefferson for his own guidance as President of the Senate from 1797 to 1801, is another recognized authority. The House has a long-standing rule that the provisions of *Jefferson's Manual* should govern the House in all applicable cases and where they are not inconsistent with the rules of the House. The House also relies on an 11-volume compilation of parliamentary precedents, entitled *Hinds' Precedents and Cannon's Precedents of the House of Representatives,* dating from 1789 to 1935, to guide its action. A later compilation, *Deschler-Brown Precedents of the House of Representatives,* spans 16 volumes and covers 1936 to date. In addition, a summary of the House precedents prior to 1959 can be found in a single volume entitled *Cannon's Procedure in the House of Representatives. Procedure in the U.S. House of Representatives,* fourth edition, as supplemented, and *House Practice,* first published in 1996 and updated in 2003, are more recent compilations of the precedents of the House, in summary form, together with other useful related material. Also, various rulings of the Chair are set out as notes in the current *House Rules and Manual.* Most parliamentary questions arising during the course of debate are responded to by a ruling based on a precedent of action in a similar situation. The Parliamentarian of the House is present in the House Chamber in order to assist the Speaker or the Chairman in making a correct ruling on parliamentary questions.

Second Reading

During general debate on a bill, an accurate account of the time used on both sides is kept and the Chairman terminates the debate when all the time allowed under the rule has been consumed. After general debate, the second reading of the bill begins. The second reading is a section-by-section reading during which time germane amendments may be offered to a section when it is read. Under many special "modified closed" rules adopted by the House, certain bills are considered as read and open only to prescribed amendments under limited time allocations. Under the normal "open" amendment process, a Member is permitted five minutes to explain the proposed amendment, after which the Member who is first recognized by the Chair is allowed to speak for five minutes in opposition to it. There is technically no further debate on that amendment, thereby effectively preventing filibuster-like tactics. This is known as the "five-minute rule". However, Members may offer an amendment to the amendment, for separate five-minute debate, or may offer a pro forma amendment—"to strike out the last word"—which does not change the language of the amendment but allows the Member five minutes for debate. Each substantive amendment and amendment thereto is put to the Committee of the Whole for adoption unless the House has adopted a special rule "self-executing" the adoption of certain amendments in the Committee of the Whole. The House may, after initially adopting an open rule, later alter that rule by unanimous consent to establish a "universe" or list of amendments to a bill. This procedure is most commonly used on general appropriation bills because of the volume of amendments.

At any time after debate has begun on proposed amendments to a section or paragraph of a bill under the five-minute rule, the Committee of the Whole may by majority vote of the Members present close debate on the amendment or the pending section or paragraph. However, if debate is closed on a section or paragraph before there has been debate on an amendment that a Member has caused to be printed in the Congressional Record at least one day prior to floor consideration of the amendment, the Member who caused the amendment to be printed in the Record is given five minutes in which to explain the amendment. Five minutes is also given to speak in opposition to the amendment and no further debate on the amendment is allowed. Amendments placed in the Congressional Record must indicate the full text of the proposed amendment, the name of the Member proposing it, the number of the bill or amendment to which it will be offered, and the point in the bill or amendment thereto where the amendment is intended to be offered. These amendments appear in the portion of the Record designated for that purpose.

Amendments and the Germaneness Rule

The rules of the House prohibit amendments of a subject matter different from the text under consideration. This rule, commonly known as the germaneness rule, is considered the single most important rule of the House of Representatives because of the obvious need to keep the focus of a body the size of the House on a predictable subject matter. The germaneness rule applies to the proceedings in the House, the Committee of the Whole, and the standing committees. There are hundreds of prior rulings or "precedents" on germaneness available to guide the Chair.

The Committee "Rises"

At the conclusion of the consideration of a bill for amendment, the Committee of the Whole "rises" and reports the bill to the House with any amendments that have been adopted. In rising, the Committee of the Whole reverts back to the House and the Chairman of the Committee is replaced in the chair by the Speaker of the House. The House then acts on the bill and any amendments adopted by the Committee of the Whole. If the Committee of the Whole rises on motion prior to the conclusion of consideration of amendments, the bill must return to the Committee of the Whole for subsequent consideration. Thus, the simple motion to rise may be used to immediately halt consideration of a bill similar to a motion to adjourn in the House.

HOUSE ACTION

Debate on a bill in the House is cut off by moving and ordering "the previous question". All debate is cut off on the bill if this motion is carried by a majority of the Members voting, a quorum being present, or by a special rule ordering the previous question upon the rising of the Committee of the Whole. The Speaker then puts the question: "Shall the bill be engrossed and read a third time?" If this question is decided in the affirmative, the bill is read a third time by title only and voted on for passage.

If the previous question has been ordered by the terms of the rule on a bill reported by the Committee of the Whole, the House immediately votes on whatever amendments have been reported by the Committee in the order in which they appear in the bill unless voted on en bloc. After completion of voting on the amendments, the House immediately votes on the passage of the bill with the amendments it has adopted. However, a motion to recommit, as described in the next section, may be offered and voted on prior to the vote on passage.

The Speaker may postpone a recorded vote on final passage of a bill or resolution or agreement to a conference report for up to two legislative days.

Measures that do not have to be considered in the Committee of the Whole are considered in the House in accordance with the terms of the rule limiting debate on the measure or under the "hour rule". The hour rule limits the amount of time that a Member may occupy in debate on a pending question to 60 minutes. Generally, the opportunity for debate may also be curtailed when the Speaker makes the rare determination that a motion is dilatory.

After passage or rejection of the bill by the House, a pro forma motion to reconsider it is automatically made and laid on the table. The motion to reconsider is tabled to prohibit this motion from being made at a later date because the vote of the House on a proposition is not final and conclusive until there has been an opportunity to reconsider it.

Motion to Recommit

After the previous question has been ordered on the passage of a bill or joint resolution, it is in order to offer one motion to recommit the bill or joint resolution to a committee and the Speaker is required to give preference in recognition for that purpose to a minority party Member who is opposed to the bill or joint resolution. This motion is normally not subject to debate. However, a motion to recommit with instructions offered after the previous question has been ordered is debatable for 10 minutes, except that the majority floor manager may demand that the debate be extended to one hour. Whatever time is allotted for debate is divided equally between the proponent and opponent of the motion. Instructions in the motion to recommit normally take the form of germane amendments proposed by the minority to immediately change the final form of the bill prior to passage. Instructions may also be "general," consisting of nonbinding instructions to the committee to take specified actions such as to "promptly" review the bill with a particular political viewpoint or to hold further hearings. Such instructions may not contain argument.

QUORUM CALLS AND ROLL CALLS

Article I, Section 5, of the Constitution provides that a majority of each House constitutes a quorum to do business and authorizes a smaller number than a quorum to compel the attendance of absent Members. In order to fulfill this constitutional responsibility, the rules of the House provide alternative procedures for quorum calls in the House and the Committee of the Whole.

In the absence of a quorum, 15 Members may initiate a call of the House to compel the attendance of absent Members. Such a call of the House must be ordered by a majority vote. A call of the House is then ordered and the call is taken by electronic device or by response to the alphabetical call of the roll of Members. Absent Members have a minimum of 15 minutes from the ordering of the call of the House by electronic device to have their presence recorded. If sufficient excuse is not offered for their absence, they may be sent for by the Sergeant-at-Arms and their attendance secured and retained. The House then determines the conditions on which they may be discharged. Members who voluntarily appear are, unless the House otherwise directs, immediately admitted to the Hall of the House and must report their names to the Clerk to be entered on the

Journal as present. Compulsory attendance or arrest of Members has been rare in modern practice.

The rules of the House provide special authority for the Speaker to recognize a Member of the Speaker's choice to move a call of the House at any time.

When a question is put to a vote by the Speaker and a quorum fails to vote on such question, if a quorum is not present and objection is made for that reason, there is a call of the House unless the House adjourns. The call is taken by electronic device and the Sergeant-at-Arms may bring in absent Members. The yeas and nays on the pending question are at the same time considered as ordered and an "automatic" recorded vote is taken. The Clerk utilizes the electronic system or calls the roll and each Member who is present may vote on the pending question. If those voting on the question and those who are present and decline to vote together make a majority of the House, the Speaker declares that a quorum is constituted and the pending question is decided as the majority of those voting have determined.

The rules of the House prohibit points of order of no quorum unless the Speaker has put a question to a vote.

The rules for quorum calls are different in some respects in the Committee of the Whole. The first time the Committee of the Whole finds itself without a quorum during a day the Chairman is required to order the roll to be called by electronic device, unless the Chairman orders a call of the Committee. However, the Chairman may refuse to entertain a point of order of no quorum during general debate. If on a call, a quorum (100 Members) appears, the Committee continues its business. If a quorum does not appear, the Committee rises and the Chairman reports the names of the absentees to the House. The rules provide for the expeditious conduct of quorum calls in the Committee of the Whole. The Chairman may suspend a quorum call after 100 Members have recorded their presence. Under such a short quorum call, the Committee will not rise and proceedings under the quorum call are vacated. In that case, a recorded vote, if ordered immediately following the termination of the short quorum call, is a minimum of 15 minutes. In the alternative, the Chair may choose to permit a full 15 minute quorum call, wherein all Members are recorded as present or absent, to be followed by a five-minute record vote on the pending question. Once a quorum of the Committee of the Whole has been established for a day, a quorum call in the Committee is only in order when the Committee is operating under the five-minute rule and the Chairman has put the pending question to a vote. The rules prohibit a point of order of no quorum against a vote in which the Committee of the Whole agrees to rise. However, an appropriate point of no quorum would be permitted against a vote defeating a motion to rise.

VOTING

There are three methods of voting in the Committee of the Whole that are also employed in the House. These are the voice vote, the division, and the recorded vote. The yea-and-nay vote is an additional method used only in the House, which may be automatic if a Member objects to the vote on the ground that a quorum is not present.

To conduct a voice vote the Chair puts the question: "As many as are in favor (as the question may be) say 'Aye'. As many as are opposed, say 'No'". The Chair determines the result on a comparison of the volume of ayes and noes. This is the form in which the vote is ordinarily taken in the first instance.

If it is difficult to determine the result of a voice vote, a division may be demanded by a Member or initiated by the Chair. The Chair then states: "As many as are in favor will rise and stand until counted". After counting those in favor he calls on those opposed to stand and be counted, thereby determining the number in favor of and those opposed to the question.

If any Member requests a recorded vote and that request is supported by at least one-fifth of a quorum of the House (44 Members), or 25 Members in the Committee of the Whole, the vote is taken by electronic device. After the recorded vote is concluded, the names of those voting and those not voting are entered in the Journal. Members have a minimum of 15 minutes to be counted from the time the record vote is ordered. The Speaker may reduce the period for voting to five minutes on subsequent votes in certain situations where there has been no intervening debate or business. The Speaker is not required to vote unless the Speaker's vote would be decisive.

The modern practice in the Committee of the Whole is to postpone and cluster votes on amendments to maximize efficient scheduling of voting. The rules of the House provide the Chairman of the Committee of the Whole discretionary authority to postpone votes on amendments and to reduce the time for voting on amendments to five minutes following a 15-minute vote on the first amendment in a series. The Chairman is not allowed to postpone votes on matters other than amendments and is mindful not to postpone votes where the outcome could be prejudicial to the offering of another amendment.

In the House, if the yeas and nays are demanded, the Speaker directs those in favor of taking the vote by that method to stand and be counted. The support of one-fifth of the Members present is necessary for ordering the yeas and nays. When the yeas and nays are ordered or a point of order is made that a quorum is not present, the Speaker states: "As many as are in favor of the proposition will vote 'Aye'." "As many as are opposed will vote 'No'." The Clerk activates the electronic system or calls the roll and reports the result to the Speaker, who announces it to the House.

The rules of the House require a three-fifths vote to pass a bill, joint resolution, amendment, or conference report that contains a specified type of federal income tax rate increase. The rules of the House also provide for automatic yeas and nays on votes on passage of certain fiscal measures including a concurrent resolution on the budget or a general appropriation bill.

The rules prohibit a Member from: (1) casting another Member's vote or recording another Member's presence in the House or the Committee of the Whole; or (2) authorizing another individual to cast a vote or record the Member's presence in the House or the Committee of the Whole.

ELECTRONIC VOTING

Recorded votes are usually taken by electronic device, except when the Speaker orders the vote to be recorded by other methods prescribed by the rules of the House, or in the failure of the electronic device to function. In addition, quorum calls are generally taken by electronic device. The electronic system works as follows: A number of vote stations are attached to selected chairs in the Chamber. Each station is equipped with a vote card slot and four indicators, marked "yea", "nay", "present", and "open" that are lit when a vote is in progress and the system is ready to accept votes. Each Member is provided with an encrypted Vote-ID Card. A Member votes by inserting the voting card into any one of the vote stations and depressing the appropriate button to indicate the Member's choice. If a Member is without a Vote-ID Card or wishes to change his vote during the last five minutes of a vote, the Member may be recorded by handing a paper ballot to the Tally Clerk, who then records the vote electronically according to the indicated preference of the Member. The paper ballots are green for "yea", red for "nay", and amber for "present".

The voting machine records the votes and reports the result when the vote is completed.

Pairing of Members

The former system of pairing of Members, where a Member could arrange in advance to be recorded as being either in favor of or opposed to the question by being "paired" with another absent Member who holds contrary views on the question, has largely been eliminated. The rules still allow for "live pairs". A live pair is where a Member votes as if not paired, subsequently withdraws that vote, and then asks to be marked "present" to protect the other Member. The most common practice is for absent Members to submit statements for the Record stating how they would have voted if present on specific votes.

System of Lights and Bells

Due to the diverse nature of daily tasks that they have to perform, it is not practicable for Members to be present in the House or Senate Chamber at every minute that the body is in session. Furthermore, many of the routine matters do not require the personal attendance of all the Members. A system consisting of electric lights and bells or buzzers located in various parts of the Capitol Building and House and Senate Office Buildings alerts Members to certain occurrences in the House and Senate Chambers.

In the House, the Speaker has ordered that the bells and lights comprising the system be utilized as follows:

1 long ring followed by a pause and then 3 rings and 3 lights on the left—Start or continuation of a notice or short quorum call in the Committee of the Whole that will be vacated if and when 100 Members appear on the floor. Bells are repeated every five minutes unless the call is vacated or the call is converted into a regular quorum call.

1 long ring and extinguishing of 3 lights on the left—Short or notice quorum call vacated.

2 rings and 2 lights on the left—15 minute recorded vote, yea-and-nay vote or automatic roll call vote by electronic device. The bells are repeated five minutes after the first ring.

2 rings and 2 lights on the left followed by a pause and then 2 more rings—Automatic roll call vote or yea-and-nay vote taken by a call of the roll in the House. The bells are repeated when the Clerk reaches the R's in the first call of the roll.

2 rings followed by a pause and then 5 rings—First vote on clustered votes. Two bells are repeated five minutes after the first ring. The first vote will take 15 minutes with successive votes at intervals of not less than five minutes. Each successive vote is signaled by five rings.

3 rings and 3 lights on the left—15 minute quorum call in either the House or in the Committee of the Whole by electronic device. The bells are repeated five minutes after the first ring.

3 rings followed by a pause and then 3 more rings—15 minute quorum call by a call of the roll. The bells are repeated when the Clerk reaches the R's in the first call of the roll.

3 rings followed by a pause and then 5 more rings—Quorum call in the Committee of the Whole that may be followed immediately by a five-minute recorded vote.

4 rings and 4 lights on the left—Adjournment of the House.

5 rings and 5 lights on the left—Any five-minute vote.

6 rings and 6 lights on the left—Recess of the House.

12 rings at 2-second intervals with 6 lights on the left—Civil Defense Warning.

The 7th light indicates that the House is in session.

Recess Authority

The House may by vote authorize the Speaker to declare a recess under the rules of the House. The Speaker also has the authority to declare the House in recess for a short time when no question is pending before the House or in the case of an emergency.

Live Coverage of Floor Proceedings

The rules of the House provide for unedited radio and television broadcasting and recording of proceedings on the floor of the House. However, the rules prohibit the use of these broadcasts and recordings for any political purpose or in any commercial advertisement. The rules of the Senate also provide for broadcasting and recording of proceedings in the Senate Chamber with similar restrictions.

XII

Congressional Budget Process

The Congressional Budget and Impoundment Control Act of 1974, as amended, provides Congress with a procedure establishing appropriate spending and revenue levels for each year. The congressional budget process, as set out in the 1974 Budget Act, is designed to coordinate decisions on sources and levels of revenues and on objects and levels of expenditures. Its basic method is to prescribe the overall size of the fiscal pie and the particular sizes of its various pieces. Each year the Congress adopts a concurrent resolution imposing overall constraints on revenues and spending and distributing the overall constraint on spending among groups of programs and activities.

Congress aims to complete action on a concurrent resolution on the budget for the next fiscal year by April

15. Congress may adopt a later budget resolution that revises the most recently adopted budget resolution. One of the mechanisms Congress uses to implement the constraints on revenue and spending is called the reconciliation process. Reconciliation is a multiple-step process designed to bring existing law in conformity with the most recently adopted concurrent resolution on the budget. The first step in the reconciliation process is the language found in a concurrent resolution on the budget instructing House and Senate committees to determine and recommend changes in laws or bills that will achieve the constraints established in the concurrent resolution on the budget. The instructions to a committee specify the amount of spending reductions or revenue changes a committee must attain and leave to the discretion of the committee the specific changes to laws or bills that must be made. The subsequent steps involve the combination of the various instructed committees' recommendations into an omnibus reconciliation bill or bills which are reported by the Committee on the Budget or by the one committee instructed, if only one committee has been instructed, and considered by the whole House. In the Senate, reconciliation bills reported from committee are entitled to expedited consideration, permitting a majority of Senators, rather than sixty, to assure consideration of the bill with limited time for amendments.

The Budget Act maintains that reconciliation provisions must be related to reconciling the budget. This principle is codified in section 313 of the Budget Act, the so-called Byrd Rule, named after Senator Robert C. Byrd of West Virginia. Section 313 provides a point of order in the Senate against extraneous matter in reconciliation bills. Determining what is extraneous is a difficult task for the Senate's Presiding Officer. The Byrd Rule may only be waived in the Senate by a three-fifths vote and sixty votes are required to overturn the presiding officer's ruling.

Congress aims to complete action on a reconciliation bill or resolution by a specified date of each year. After Congress has completed action on a concurrent resolution on the budget for a fiscal year, it is generally not in order to consider legislation that does not conform to the constraints on spending and revenue set out in the resolution.

The Unfunded Mandates Reform Act of 1995, through an amendment to the Congressional Budget Act, established requirements on committees with respect to measures containing unfunded intergovernmental mandates. An unfunded intergovernmental mandate is the imposition of a substantial financial requirement or obligation on a state, local, or tribal government. The Act also established a unique point of order to enforce the requirements of the Act with respect to intergovernmental mandates in excess of fifty million dollars annually. In the House, an unfunded mandate point of order is not disposed of by a ruling of the Chair but by the Chair putting the question of consideration to the body. The House or the Committee of the Whole then decides by vote whether or not to proceed with the measure with the alleged mandate contained therein.

XIII

Engrossment and Message to Senate

The preparation of a copy of the bill in the form in which it has passed the House can be a detailed and complicated process because of the large number and complexity of amendments to some bills adopted by the House. Frequently, these amendments are offered during a spirited debate with little or no prior formal preparation. The amendment may be for the purpose of inserting new language, substituting different words for those set out in the bill, or deleting portions of the bill. It is not unusual to have more than 100 amendments adopted, including those proposed by the committee at the time the bill is reported and those offered from the floor during the consideration of the bill in the Chamber. In some cases, amendments offered from the floor are written in longhand. Each amendment must be inserted in precisely the proper place in the bill, with the spelling and punctuation exactly as it was adopted by the House. It is extremely important that the Senate receive a copy of the bill in the precise form in which it has passed the House. The preparation of such a copy is the function of the enrolling clerk.

In the House, the enrolling clerk is under the Clerk of the House. In the Senate, the enrolling clerk is under the Secretary of the Senate. The enrolling clerk receives all the papers relating to the bill, including the official Clerk's copy of the bill as reported by the standing committee and each amendment adopted by the House.

From this material, the enrolling clerk prepares the engrossed copy of the bill as passed, containing all the amendments agreed to by the House. At this point, the measure ceases technically to be called a bill and is termed "An Act" signifying that it is the act of one body of the Congress, although it is still popularly referred to as a bill. The engrossed bill is printed on blue paper and is signed by the Clerk of the House. Bills may also originate in the Senate with certain exceptions. For a discussion of bills originating in the Senate, see Part XVI.

XIV

SENATE ACTION

The Parliamentarian, in the name of the Vice President, as the President of the Senate, refers the engrossed bill to the appropriate standing committee of the Senate in conformity with the rules of the Senate. The bill is reprinted immediately and copies are made available in the document rooms of both Houses. This printing is known as the "Act print" or the "Senate referred print".

COMMITTEE CONSIDERATION

Senate committees give the bill the same detailed consideration as it received in the House and may report it with or without amendment. A committee member who wishes to express an individual view or a group of Members who wish to file a minority report may do so by giving notice, at the time of the approval of a report on the measure, of an intention to file supplemental, minority, or additional views. These views may be filed within three days with the clerk of the committee and become a part of the report. When a committee reports a bill, it is reprinted with the committee amendments indicated by showing new matter in italics and deleted matter in line-through type. The calendar number and report number are indicated on the first and back pages, together with the name of the Senator making the report. The committee report and any minority or individual views accompanying the bill also are printed at the same time.

All committee meetings, including those to conduct hearings, must be open to the public. However, a majority of the members of a committee or subcommittee may, after discussion in closed session, vote in open session to close a meeting or series of meetings on the same subject for no longer than 14 days if it is determined that the matters to be discussed or testimony to be taken will disclose matters necessary to be kept secret in the interests of national defense or the confidential conduct of the foreign relations of the United States; will relate solely to internal committee staff management or procedure; will tend to charge an individual with a crime or misconduct, to disgrace or injure the professional standing of an individual, or otherwise to expose an individual to public contempt, or will represent a clearly unwarranted invasion of the privacy of an individual; will disclose law enforcement information that is required to be kept secret; will disclose certain information regarding certain trade secrets; or may disclose matters required to be kept confidential under other provisions of law or government regulation.

CHAMBER PROCEDURE

The rules of procedure in the Senate differ to a large extent from those in the House. The Senate relies heavily on the practice of obtaining unanimous consent for actions to be taken. For example, at the time that a bill is reported, the Majority Leader may ask unanimous consent for the immediate consideration of the bill. If the bill is of a noncontroversial nature and there is no objection, the Senate may pass the bill with little or no debate and with only a brief explanation of its purpose and effect. Even in this instance, the bill is subject to amendment by any Senator. A simple majority vote is necessary to carry an amendment as well as to pass the bill. If there is any objection, the report must lie over one legislative day and the bill is placed on the calendar.

Measures reported by standing committees of the Senate may not be considered unless the report of that committee has been available to Senate Members for at least two days (excluding Sundays and legal holidays) prior to consideration of the measure in the Senate. This requirement, however, may be waived by agreement of the Majority and Minority leaders and does not apply in certain emergency situations.

In the Senate, measures are brought up for consideration by a simple unanimous consent request, by a complex unanimous consent agreement, or by a motion to proceed to the consideration of a measure on the calendar. A unanimous consent agreement, sometimes referred to as a "time agreement", makes the consideration of a measure in order and often limits the amount of debate that will take place on the measure and lists the amendments that will be considered. The offering of a unanimous consent request to consider a measure or the offering of a motion to proceed to the consideration of a measure is reserved, by tradition, to the Majority Leader.

Usually a motion to consider a measure on the calendar is made only when unanimous consent to consider the measure cannot be obtained. There are two calendars in the Senate, the Calendar of Business and the Executive Calendar. All legislation is placed on the Calendar of Business and treaties and nominations are placed on the Executive Calendar. Unlike the House, there is no differentiation on the Calendar of Business between the treatment of: (1) bills raising revenue, general appropriation bills, and bills of a public character appropriating money or property; and (2) other bills of a public character not appropriating money or property.

The rules of the Senate provide that at the conclusion of the morning business for each "legislative day" the Senate proceeds to the consideration of the calendar. In the Senate, the term "legislative day" means the period of time from when the Senate adjourns until the next time the Senate adjourns. Because the Senate often "recesses" rather than "adjourns" at the end of a daily session, the legislative day usually does not correspond to the 24-hour period comprising a calendar day. Thus, a legislative day may cover a long period of time—from days to weeks, or even months. Because of this and the modern practice of waiving the call of the calendar by unanimous consent at the start of a new legislative day, it is rare to have a call of the calendar. When the calendar is called, bills that are not objected to are taken up in their order, and each Senator is entitled to speak once and for five minutes only on any question. Objection may be interposed at any stage of the proceedings, but on motion the Senate may continue consideration after the call of the calendar is completed, and the limitations on debate then do not apply.

On any day (other than a Monday that begins a new legislative day), following the announcement of the close of morning business, any Senator, usually the Majority Leader, obtaining recognition may move to take up any bill out of its regular order on the calendar. The five-minute limitation on debate does not apply to the consideration of a bill taken up in this manner, and debate may continue until the hour when the Presiding Officer of the Senate "lays down" the unfinished business of the day. At that point consideration of the bill is discontinued and the measure reverts back to the Calendar of Business and may again be called up at another time under the same conditions.

When a bill has been objected to and passed over on the call of the calendar it is not necessarily lost. The Majority Leader, after consulting the Minority Leader, determines the time at which the bill will be considered.

At that time, a motion is made to consider the bill. The motion is debatable if made after the morning hour.

Once a Senator is recognized by the Presiding Officer, the Senator may speak for as long as the Senator wishes and loses the floor only when the Senator yields it or takes certain parliamentary actions that forfeit the Senator's right to the floor. However, a Senator may not speak more than twice on any one question in debate on the same legislative day without leave of the Senate. Debate ends when a Senator yields the floor and no other Senator seeks recognition, or when a unanimous consent agreement limiting the time of debate is operating.

On occasion, Senators opposed to a measure may extend debate by making lengthy speeches or a number of speeches at various stages of consideration intended to prevent or defeat action on the measure. This is the tactic known as "filibustering". Debate, however, may be closed if 16 Senators sign a motion to that effect and the motion is carried by three-fifths of the Senators duly chosen and sworn. Such a motion is voted on one hour after the Senate convenes, following a quorum call on the next day after a day of session has intervened. This procedure is called "invoking cloture". In 1986, the Senate amended its rules to limit "post-cloture" consideration to 30 hours. A Senator may speak for not more than one hour and may yield all or a part of that time to the majority or minority floor managers of the bill under consideration or to the Majority or Minority leader. The Senate may increase the time for "post-cloture" debate by a vote of three-fifths of the Senators duly chosen and sworn. After the time for debate has expired, the Senate may consider only amendments actually pending before voting on the bill.

While a measure is being considered it is subject to amendment and each amendment, including those proposed by the committee that reported the bill, is considered separately. Generally, there is no requirement that proposed amendments be germane to the subject matter of the bill except in the case of general appropriation bills or where "cloture" has been invoked. Under the rules, a "rider", an amendment proposing substantive legislation to an appropriation bill, is prohibited. However, this prohibition may be suspended by two-thirds vote on a motion to permit consideration of such an amendment on one day's notice in writing. Debate must be germane during the first three hours after business is laid down unless determined to the contrary by unanimous consent or on motion without debate. After final action on the amendments the bill is ready for engrossment and the third reading, which is by title only. The Presiding Officer then puts the question on the passage and a voice vote is usually taken although a yea-and-nay vote is in order if demanded by one-fifth of the Senators present. A simple majority is necessary for passage. Before an amended measure is cleared for its return to the House of Representatives, or an unamended measure is cleared for enrollment, a Senator who voted with the prevailing side, or who abstained from voting, may make a motion within the next two days to reconsider the action. If the measure was passed without a recorded vote, any Senator may make the motion to reconsider. That motion is usually tabled and its tabling constitutes a final determination. If, however, the motion is granted, the Senate, by majority vote, may either affirm its action, which then becomes final, or reverse it.

The original engrossed House bill, together with the engrossed Senate amendments, if any, or the original engrossed Senate bill, as the case may be, is then returned to the House with a message stating the action taken by the Senate. Where the Senate has adopted amendments, the message requests that the House concur in them.

For a more detailed discussion of Senate procedure, see *Enactment of a Law*, by Robert B. Dove, former Parliamentarian of the Senate.

XV

FINAL ACTION ON AMENDED BILL

On their return to the House, the official papers relating to the amended measure are placed on the Speaker's table to await House action on the Senate amendments. Although rarely exercised, the Speaker has the authority to refer Senate amendments to the appropriate committee or committees with or without time limits on their consideration. If the amendments are of a minor or noncontroversial nature, any Member, usually the chairman of a committee that reported the bill, may, at the direction of the committee, ask unanimous consent to take the bill with the amendments from the Speaker's table and agree to the Senate amendments. At this point, the Clerk reads the title of the bill and the Senate amendments. If there is no objection, the amendments are then declared to be agreed to, and the bill is ready to be enrolled for presentation to the President. If unanimous consent is not obtainable, the few bills that do not require consideration in the Committee of the Whole are privileged and may be called up from the Speaker's table by motion for immediate consideration of the amendments. A simple majority is necessary to carry the motion and thereby complete floor action on the measure. A Senate amendment to a House bill is subject to a point of order that it must first be considered in the Committee of the Whole, if, originating in the House, it would be subject to that point of order. Most Senate amendments require consideration in the Committee of the Whole and this procedure by privileged motion is seldom utilized.

Request for a Conference

The mere fact that each House may have separately passed its own bill on a subject is not sufficient to make either bill eligible for conference. One House must first take the additional step of amending and then passing the bill of the other House to form the basis for a conference. If the amendments of the Senate are substantial or controversial, a Member, usually the chairman of the committee of jurisdiction, may request unanimous consent to take the House bill with the Senate amendments from the Speaker's table, disagree to the amendments and request or agree to a conference with the Senate to resolve the disagreeing votes of the two Houses. In the case of a Senate bill with House amendments, the House may insist on the House amendments and request a conference. For a discussion of bills originating in the Senate, see Part XVI. If there is objection, the Speaker may recognize a Member for a motion, if offered by the direction of the primary committee and of all reporting committees that had initial referral of the bill, to: (1) disagree to the Senate amendments and ask for or agree to a conference; or (2) insist on the House amendments to a Senate bill and request or agree to a conference. This may also be accomplished by a motion to suspend the rules with a two-thirds vote or by a rule from the Committee on Rules. If there is no objection to the request, or if the motion is carried, a motion to instruct the managers of the conference would be in order. This initial motion to instruct is the prerogative of the minority party. The instructions to conferees usually urge the managers to accept or reject a particular Senate or House provision or to take a more generally described political position to the extent possible within the scope of the conference. However, such instructions may not contain argument and are not binding on House or Senate conferees. After the motion to instruct is disposed of, the Speaker then appoints the managers, informally known as conferees, on the part of the House and a message is sent to the Senate advising it of the House action. A majority of the Members appointed to be conferees must have been supporters of the House position, as determined by the Speaker. The Speaker must appoint Members primarily responsible for the legislation and must include, to the fullest extent feasible, the principal proponents of the major provisions of the bill as it passed the House. The Speaker usually follows the suggestion of the committee chairman in designating the conferees on the part of the House from among the members of the committee with jurisdiction over the House or Senate provisions. Occasionally, the Speaker appoints conferees from more than one committee and may specify the portions of the House and Senate versions to which they are assigned. The number is fixed by the Speaker and majority party representation generally reflects the ratio for the full House committee, but may be greater on important bills. The Speaker also has the authority to name substitute conferees on specific provisions and add or remove conferees after his original appointment. Representation of both major parties is an important attribute of all our parliamentary procedures but, in the case of conference committees, it is important that the views of the House on matters in conference be properly represented.

If the Senate agrees to the request for a conference, a similar committee is appointed by unanimous consent by the Presiding Officer of the Senate. Both political parties may be represented on the Senate conference committee. The Senate and House committees need not be the same size but each House has one vote in conference as determined by a majority within each set or subset of conferees.

The request for a conference may only be made by the body in possession of the official papers. Occasionally, the Senate, anticipating that the House will not concur in its amendments, votes to insist on its amendments and requests a conference on passage of the bill prior to returning the bill to the House. This practice serves to expedite the matter because time may be saved by the designation of the Senate conferees before returning the bill to the House. The matter of which body requests the conference is not without significance because the body asking for the conference normally acts last on the report to be submitted by the conferees and a motion to recommit the conference report is not available to the body that acts last.

AUTHORITY OF CONFEREES

The conference committee is sometimes popularly referred to as the "Third House of Congress". Although the managers on the part of each House meet together as one committee they are in effect two separate committees, each of which votes separately and acts by a majority vote. For this reason, the number of managers from each House is largely immaterial.

The House conferees are strictly limited in their consideration to matters in disagreement between the two Houses. Consequently, they may not strike out or amend any portion of the bill that was not amended by the other House. Furthermore, they may not insert new matter that is not germane to or that is beyond the scope of the differences between the two Houses. Where the Senate amendment revises a figure or an amount contained in the bill, the conferees are limited to the difference between the two numbers and may neither increase the greater nor decrease the smaller figure. Neither House may alone, by instructions, empower its managers to make a change in the text to which both Houses have agreed.

When a disagreement to an amendment in the nature of a substitute is committed to a conference committee, managers on the part of the House may propose a substitute that is a germane modification of the matter in disagreement, but the introduction of any language in that substitute presenting specific additional matter not committed to the conference committee by either House is not in order. Moreover, their report may not include matter not committed to the conference committee by either House. The report may not include a modification of any specific matter committed to the conference committee by either or both Houses if that modification is beyond the scope of that specific matter as committed to the conference committee.

Under a recent reassertion of a Senate rule, Senate conferees are bound to consider only those matters that bare a certain relevancy to a House or Senate provision in conference.

The managers on the part of the House are under specific guidelines when in conference on general appropriation bills. An amendment by the Senate to a general appropriation bill which would be in violation of the rules of the House, if such amendment had originated in the House, including an amendment changing existing law, providing appropriations not authorized by law, or providing reappropriations of unexpended balances, or an amendment by the Senate providing for an appropriation on a bill other than a general appropriation bill, may not be agreed to by the managers on the part of the House. However, the House may grant specific authority to agree to such an amendment by a separate vote on a motion to instruct on each specific amendment.

MEETINGS AND ACTION OF CONFEREES

The rules of the House require that one conference meeting be open, unless the House, in open session, determines by a vote of the yeas and nays that a meeting will be closed to the public. When the report of the conference committee is read in the House, a point of order may be made that the conferees failed to comply with the House rule requiring an open conference meeting. If the point of order is sustained, the conference report is considered rejected by the House and a new conference is deemed to have been requested.

There are generally four forms of recommendations available to the conferees when reporting back to their bodies:

(1) The Senate recede from all (or certain of) its amendments.

(2) The House recede from its disagreement to all (or certain of) the Senate amendments and agree thereto.

(3) The House recede from its disagreement to all (or certain of) the Senate amendments and agree thereto with amendments.

(4) The House recede from all (or certain of) its amendments to the Senate amendments or its amendments to Senate bill.

In most instances, the result of the conference is a compromise growing out of the third type of recommendation available to the conferees because one House has originally substituted its own bill to be considered as a single amendment. The complete report may be composed of any one or more of these recommendations with respect to the various amendments where there are numbered amendments. In earlier practice, on general appropriation bills with numbered Senate amendments, because of the special rules preventing House conferees from agreeing to Senate amendments changing existing law or appropriations not authorized by law, the conferees often found themselves, under the rules or in fact, unable to reach an agreement with respect to one or more amendments and reported back a statement of their inability to agree on those particular amendments. These amendments were acted upon separately. This partial disagreement is not practicable where, as in current practice, the Senate strikes out all after the enacting clause and substitutes its own bill that must be considered as a single amendment.

If they are unable to reach any agreement whatsoever, the conferees report that fact to their respective bodies and the amendments may be disposed of by motion. Usually, new conferees may be appointed in either or both Houses. In addition, the Houses may provide a new nonbinding instruction to the conferees as to the position they are to take.

After House conferees on any bill or resolution in conference between the two bodies have been appointed for 20 calendar days and 10 legislative days and have failed to make a report, a motion to instruct the House conferees, or discharge them and appoint new conferees is privileged. The motion can be made only after the Member announces his intention to offer the motion and only at a time designated by the Speaker in the legislative schedule of the following day. Like the initial motion to instruct, the 20-day motion may not contain argument and must remain within the scope of conference. In addition, during the last six days of a session, it is a privileged motion to move to discharge, appoint, or instruct House conferees after House conferees have been appointed 36 hours without having made a report.

Conference Reports

When the conferees, by majority vote of each group, have reached complete agreement or find that they are able to agree with respect to some but not all separately numbered amendments, they make their recommendations in a report made in duplicate that must be signed by a majority of the conferees appointed by each body on each provision to which they are appointed. The minority of the managers have no authority to file a statement of minority views in connection with the conference report. The report is required to be printed in both Houses and must be accompanied by an explanatory statement prepared jointly by the conferees on the part of the House and the conferees on the part of the Senate. The statement must be sufficiently detailed and explicit to inform Congress of the effects of the report on the matters committed to conference. The engrossed bill and amendments and one copy of the report are delivered to the body that is to act first on the report, usually, the body that agreed to the conference requested by the other.

In the Senate, the presentation of a conference report always is in order except when the Journal is being read, a point of order or motion to adjourn is pending, or while the Senate is voting or ascertaining the presence of a quorum. When the report is received, the question of proceeding to the consideration of the report, if raised, is immediately voted on without debate. The report is not subject to amendment in either body and must be accepted or rejected as an entirety. If the time for debate on the adoption of the report is limited, the time allotted must be equally divided between the majority and minority party. The Senate, acting first, prior to voting on agreeing to the report may by majority vote order it recommitted to the conferees. When the Senate agrees to the report, its managers are thereby discharged and it then delivers the original papers to the House with a message advising that body of its action.

A report that contains any recommendations which extend beyond the scope of differences between the two

Houses is subject to a point of order in its entirety unless that point of order is waived in the House by unanimous consent, adoption of a rule reported from the Committee on Rules, or the suspension of the rules by a two-thirds vote. In the Senate, a report exceeding the scope of conference is likewise subject to a point of order and the Chair will use a relevancy standard in testing the relationship of a targeted provision to matter in the House or Senate version.

The presentation of a conference report in the House is in order at any time, except during a reading of the Journal or the conduct of a record vote, a vote by division, or a quorum call. The report is considered in the House and may not be sent to the Committee of the Whole on the suggestion that it contains matters ordinarily requiring consideration in that Committee. The report may not be received by the House if the required joint statement does not accompany it.

However, it is not in order to consider either: (1) a conference report; or (2) a motion to dispose of a Senate amendment (including an amendment in the nature of a substitute) reported in disagreement by a conference committee, until the third calendar day (excluding Saturdays, Sundays, and legal holidays unless the House is in session on those days) after the report and accompanying statement have been filed in the House and made available to the Members in the Congressional Record. However, these provisions do not apply during the last six days of the session. It is also not in order to consider a conference report or a motion to dispose of a Senate amendment reported in disagreement unless copies of the report and accompanying statement, together with the text of the amendment, have been available to Members for at least two hours before their consideration. By contrast, it is always in order to call up for consideration a report from the Committee on Rules on the same day reported that proposes only to waive the availability requirements for a conference report or a Senate amendment reported in disagreement. The time allotted for debate on a conference report or motion is one hour, equally divided between the majority party and the minority party. However, if the majority and minority floor managers both support the conference report or motion, one-third of the debate time must be allotted to a Member who is opposed. If the House does not agree to a conference report that the Senate has already agreed to, the report may not be recommitted to conference. In that situation, the Senate conferees are discharged when the Senate agrees to the report. The House may then request a new conference with the Senate and conferees must be reappointed.

If a conference report is called up before the House containing matter which would be in violation of the rules of the House with respect to germaneness if the matter had been offered as an amendment in the House, and which is contained either: (1) in the Senate bill or Senate amendment to the House measure (including a Senate amendment in the nature of a substitute for the text of that measure as passed by the House) and accepted by the House conferees or agreed to by the conference committee with modification; or (2) in a substitute amendment agreed to by the conference committee, a point of order may be made at the beginning of consideration that nongermane matter is contained in the report. The point of order may also be waived by a special rule. If the point of order is sustained, a motion to reject the nongermane matter identified by the point of order is privileged. The motion is debatable for 40 minutes, one-half of the time in favor of, and one-half in opposition to, the motion. Notwithstanding the final disposition of a point of order made with respect to the report, or of a motion to reject nongermane matter, further points of order may be made with respect to the report, and further motions may be made to reject other nongermane matter in the conference report not covered by any previous point of order which has been sustained. If a motion to reject has been adopted, after final disposition of all points of order and motions to reject, the conference report is considered rejected and the question then pending before the House is whether: (1) to recede and concur with an amendment that consists of that portion of the conference report not rejected; or (2) to insist on the House amendment. If all motions to reject are defeated and the House thereby decides to permit the inclusion of the nongermane Senate matter in the conference report, then, after the allocation of time for debate on the conference report, it is in order to move the previous question on the adoption of the conference report.

Similar procedures are available in the House when the Senate proposes an amendment to a measure that would be in violation of the rule against nongermane amendments, and thereafter it is (1) reported in disagreement by a committee of conference or (2) before the House and the stage of disagreement is reached.

The numbered amendments of the Senate reported in disagreement may be voted on separately and may be adopted by a majority vote after the adoption of the conference report itself as though no conference had been had with respect to those amendments. The Senate may recede from all amendments, or from certain of its amendments, insisting on the others with or without a request for a further conference with respect to them. If the House does not accept the amendments insisted on by the Senate, the entire conference process may begin again with respect to them. One House may also further amend an amendment of the other House until the third degree stage of amendment within that House is reached.

CUSTODY OF PAPERS

The custody of the original official papers is important in conference procedure because either body may act on a conference report only when in possession of the papers. The papers are transmitted to the body agreeing to the conference and from that body to the managers of the House that asked for the conference. The latter in turn carry the papers with them to the conference and at its conclusion turn them over to the managers of the

House that agreed to the conference. The managers of the House that agreed to the conference deliver them to their own House, that acts first on the report, and then delivers the papers to the other House for final action on the report. However, if the managers on the part of House asking for the conference, the report may be acted on first by the House asking for the conference.

At the conclusion of the conference, each group of conferees retains one copy of the report that has been made in duplicate and signed by a majority of the managers of each body. The House copy is signed first by the House managers and the Senate copy is signed first by its managers.

A bill cannot become a law of the land until it has been approved in identical form by both Houses of Congress. When the bill has finally been approved by both Houses, all the original papers are transmitted to the enrolling clerk of the body in which the bill originated.

XVI

BILL ORIGINATING IN SENATE

The preceding discussion has described the legislative process for bills originating in the House. When a bill originates in the Senate, this process is reversed. When the Senate passes a bill that originated in the Senate, it is sent to the House for consideration unless it is held by unanimous consent to become a vehicle for a similar House bill if and when passed by the House. The Senate bill is referred to the appropriate House committee for consideration or held at the Speaker's table at the Speaker's discretion for possible amendment following action on a companion House bill. If the committee reports the bill to the full House and if the bill is passed by the House without amendment, it is ready for enrollment. If the House passes an amended version of the Senate bill, the bill is returned to the Senate for action on the House amendments. The Senate may agree to the amendments or request a conference to resolve the disagreement over the House amendments or may further amend the House amendments. In accordance with the Constitution, the Senate cannot originate revenue measures. By tradition, the House also originates general appropriation bills. If the Senate does originate a revenue measure either as a Senate bill or an amendment to a non-revenue House bill, it can be returned to the Senate by a vote of the House as an infringement of the constitutional prerogative of the House.

XVII

Enrollment

When the bill has been agreed to in identical form by both bodies—either: (1) without amendment by the Senate; (2) by House concurrence in Senate amendments; (3) by Senate concurrence in House amendments; or (4) by agreement in both bodies to the conference report—a copy of the bill is enrolled for presentation to the President.

The preparation of the enrolled bill is a painstaking and important task because it must reflect precisely the effect of all amendments, either by way of deletion, substitution, or addition, agreed to by both bodies. The enrolling clerk of the House, with respect to bills originating in the House, receives the original engrossed bill, the engrossed Senate amendments, the signed conference report, the several messages from the Senate, and a notation of the final action by the House, for the purpose of preparing the enrolled copy. From these documents, the enrolling clerk must meticulously prepare for presentation to the President the final form of the bill as it was agreed to by both Houses. On occasion, as many as 500 amendments have been adopted, each of which must be set out in the enrollment exactly as agreed to, and all punctuation must be in accord with the action taken.

The enrolled bill is printed on parchment paper and certified by the Clerk of the House stating that the bill originated in the House of Representatives. A bill originating in the Senate is examined and certified by the Secretary of the Senate. A House bill is then examined for accuracy by the Clerk. When he is satisfied with the accuracy of the bill, he attaches a slip stating that it finds the bill truly enrolled and sends it to the Speaker of the House for signature. All bills, regardless of the body in which they originated, are signed first by the Speaker and then by the Vice President of the United States, who, under the Constitution, serves as the President of the Senate. The President pro tempore of the Senate may also sign enrolled bills. The Speaker of the House may sign enrolled bills whether or not the House is in session. The President of the Senate may sign bills only while the Senate is actually sitting but advance permission is normally granted to sign during a recess or after adjournment. If the Speaker or the President of the Senate is unable to sign the bill, it may be signed by an authorized Member of the respective House. After both signatures are affixed, a House bill is returned to the Clerk for presentation to the President for action under the Constitution. A Senate bill is presented to the President by the Secretary of the Senate.

XVIII

PRESIDENTIAL ACTION

Article I, Section 7, of the Constitution provides in part that—

> Every Bill which shall have passed the House of Representatives and the Senate, shall, before it becomes a Law, be presented to the President of the United States.

In actual practice, the Clerk, or the Secretary of the Senate when the bill originated in that body, delivers the original enrolled bill to a clerk at the White House and obtains a receipt. The fact of the delivery is then reported to the House by the Clerk. Delivery to a White House clerk has customarily been regarded as presentation to the President and as commencing the 10-day constitutional period for presidential action.

Copies of the enrolled bill usually are transmitted by the White House to the various departments interested in the subject matter so that they may advise the President on the issues surrounding the bill.

If the President approves the bill, he signs it and usually writes the word "approved" and the date. However, the Constitution requires only that the President sign it.

The bill may become law without the President's signature by virtue of the constitutional provision that if the President does not return a bill with objections within 10 days (excluding Sundays) after it has been presented to the President, it becomes law as if the President had signed it. However, if Congress by their adjournment prevent its return, it does not become law. This is known as a "pocket veto"; that is, the bill does not become law even though the President has not sent his objections to the Congress. The Congress has interpreted the President's ability to pocket veto a bill to be limited to final adjournment "sine die" of a Congress where Congress has finally prevented return by the originating House and not to interim adjournments or first session adjournments where the originating House of Congress through its agents is able to receive a veto message for subsequent reconsideration by that Congress when it reconvenes. The extent of pocket veto authority has not been definitively decided by the courts.

Notice of the signing of a bill by the President is sent by message to the House in which it originated and that House informs the other, although this action is not necessary for the act to be valid. The action is also noted in the Congressional Record.

A bill becomes law on the date of approval or passage over the President's veto, unless it expressly provides a different effective date.

Veto Message

By the terms of the Constitution, if the President does not approve the bill "he shall return it, with his Objections to that House in which it shall have originated, who shall enter the Objections at large on their Journal, and proceed to reconsider it". A bill returned with the President's objections, need not be voted on at once when laid before the House since the vetoed bill can be postponed, referred back to committee, or tabled before the question on passage is pending. A vetoed bill is always privileged until directly voted upon, and a motion to take it from the table or from committee is in order at any time.

Once the relevant Member moves the previous question on the question of override, the question is then put by the Speaker as follows: "Will the House on reconsideration agree to pass the bill, the objections of the President to the contrary notwithstanding?" Under the Constitution, a vote by the yeas and nays is required to pass a bill over the President's veto. The Clerk activates the electronic system or calls the roll with those in favor of passing the bill answering "Aye", and those opposed "No". If fewer than two-thirds of the Members present vote in the affirmative, a quorum being present, the bill is rejected, and a message is sent to the Senate advising that body of the House action. However, if two-thirds vote in the affirmative, the bill is sent with the President's objections to the Senate, unless that body has acted first, together with a message advising it of the action in the House.

The procedure in the Senate is the same as a two-thirds affirmative vote is also necessary to pass the bill over the President's objections. If the Senate joins the House and votes two-thirds in the affirmative to pass the bill, the measure becomes the law of the land notwithstanding the objections of the President, and it is ready for publication as a binding statute.

LINE ITEM VETO

From 1997 until it was declared unconstitutional in 1998, the Line Item Veto Act provided the President authority to cancel certain individual items contained in a bill or joint resolution that he had signed into law. The law allowed the President to cancel only three types of fiscal items: a dollar amount of discretionary budget authority, an item of new direct spending, and a tax change benefiting a class of 100 or fewer. While the Act has not been repealed, the Supreme Court in *Clinton v. City of New York*, 118 S. Ct. 2091 (1998), struck down the Line Item Veto Act as unconstitutional.

XIX

Publication

One of the important steps in the enactment of a valid law is the requirement that it shall be made known to the people who are to be bound by it. There would be no justice if the state were to hold its people responsible for their conduct before it made known to them the unlawfulness of such behavior. In practice, our laws are published immediately upon their enactment so that the public will be aware of them.

If the President approves a bill, or allows it to become law without signing it, the original enrolled bill is sent from the White House to the Archivist of the United States for publication. If a bill is passed by both Houses over the objections of the President, the body that last overrides the veto transmits it. It is then assigned a public law number, and paginated for the Statutes at Large volume covering that session of Congress. The public and private law numbers run in sequence starting anew at the beginning of each Congress and are prefixed for ready identification by the number of the Congress. For example, the first public law of the 108th Congress is designated Public Law 108–1 and the first private law of the 108th Congress is designated Private Law 108–1. Subsequent laws of this Congress also will contain the same prefix designator.

SLIP LAWS

The first official publication of the statute is in the form generally known as the "slip law". In this form, each law is published separately as an unbound pamphlet. The heading indicates the public or private law number, the date of approval, and the bill number. The heading of a slip law for a public law also indicates the United States Statutes at Large citation. If the statute has been passed over the veto of the President, or has become law without the President's signature because he did not return it with objections, an appropriate statement is inserted instead of the usual notation of approval.

The Office of the Federal Register, National Archives and Records Administration prepares the slip laws and provides marginal editorial notes giving the citations to laws mentioned in the text and other explanatory details. The marginal notes also give the United States Code classifications, enabling the reader immediately to determine where the statute will appear in the Code. Each slip law also includes an informative guide to the legislative history of the law consisting of the committee report number, the name of the committee in each

House, as well as the date of consideration and passage in each House, with a reference to the Congressional Record by volume, year, and date. A reference to presidential statements relating to the approval of a bill or the veto of a bill when the veto was overridden and the bill becomes law is included in the legislative history as a citation to the Weekly Compilation of Presidential Documents.

Copies of the slip laws are delivered to the document rooms of both Houses where they are available to officials and the public. They may also be obtained by annual subscription or individual purchase from the Government Printing Office and are available in electronic form. Section 113 of title 1 of the United States Code provides that slip laws are competent evidence in all the federal and state courts, tribunals, and public offices.

STATUTES AT LARGE

The United States Statutes at Large, prepared by the Office of the Federal Register, National Archives and Records Administration, provide a permanent collection of the laws of each session of Congress in bound volumes. The latest volume containing the laws of the first session of the 107th Congress is number 115 in the series. Each volume contains a complete index and a table of contents. A legislative history appears at the end of each law. There are also extensive marginal notes referring to laws in earlier volumes and to earlier and later matters in the same volume.

Under the provisions of a statute originally enacted in 1895, these volumes are legal evidence of the laws contained in them and will be accepted as proof of those laws in any court in the United States.

The Statutes at Large are a chronological arrangement of the laws exactly as they have been enacted. The laws are not arranged according to subject matter and do not reflect the present status of an earlier law that has been amended. The laws are organized in that manner in the code of laws.

UNITED STATES CODE

The United States Code contains a consolidation and codification of the general and permanent laws of the United States arranged according to subject matter under 50 title headings, largely in alphabetical order. It sets out the current status of the laws, as amended, without repeating all the language of the amendatory acts except where necessary. The Code is declared to be prima facie evidence of those laws. Its purpose is to present the laws in a concise and usable form without requiring recourse to the many volumes of the Statutes at Large containing the individual amendments.

The Code is prepared by the Law Revision Counsel of the House of Representatives. New editions are published every six years and cumulative supplements are published after the conclusion of each regular session of the Congress. The Code is also available in electronic format on CD-ROM and the Internet.

Twenty-four of the 50 titles have been revised and enacted into positive law, and one title has been eliminated by consolidation with another title. Titles that have been revised and enacted into positive law are legal evidence of the law and may be updated by direct amendment. Eventually all the titles will be revised and enacted into positive law.

www.ingramcontent.com/pod-product-compliance
Lightning Source LLC
LaVergne TN
LVHW020642100826
845148LV00012B/2298

* 9 7 8 0 9 8 2 6 2 6 6 0 3 *